A HAMLYN POINTER BOOK

PREHISTORIC MAN

 A HAMLYN POINTER BOOK

PREHISTORIC MAN

By Anthony Harvey

Illustrated by A. Oxenham

HAMLYN
LONDON · NEW YORK · SYDNEY · TORONTO

**The illustrations in this book have been
selected from the Hamlyn all-colour paperback
FOSSIL MAN by Michael H. Day**

Published 1972 by
The Hamlyn Publishing Group Limited
London · New York · Sydney · Toronto
Hamlyn House, Feltham, Middlesex, England
© Copyright The Hamlyn Publishing Group Limited 1972
ISBN 0 600 33461 9
Printed by Officine Grafiche Arnoldo Mondadori,
Verona, Italy

Contents

The World of Prehistoric Man 6
Finding Fossil Man 11
Dating the Finds 16
The Framework of Man 22
Man and the Animal Kingdom 32
The Ancestors of Man 39
The Culture of Man 61
Index 74

THE WORLD OF PREHISTORIC MAN

Any member of a community who was born over one hundred years ago is viewed with awe and respect. Even so, it is difficult to imagine this earlier period of time, an age which was without motor cars and buses, wireless and television, aeroplanes and space ships. The changes occurring during this time have been enormous, so far as human beings are concerned.

A thousand years ago there were no large towns, the island continent of Australia was known only to its native inhabitants, and Vikings were gradually exploring and settling lands in the north Atlantic – in the Faroes, Greenland, and parts of North America. Still, the people themselves would have been easily recognizable as our own species, and the hills, valleys, and untouched land would be much the same as now.

These spans of time, large though they may be to the human mind, are negligible when compared to geological time. Our planet is estimated to be about 5,000 million years old, but it has undergone many changes since its formation.

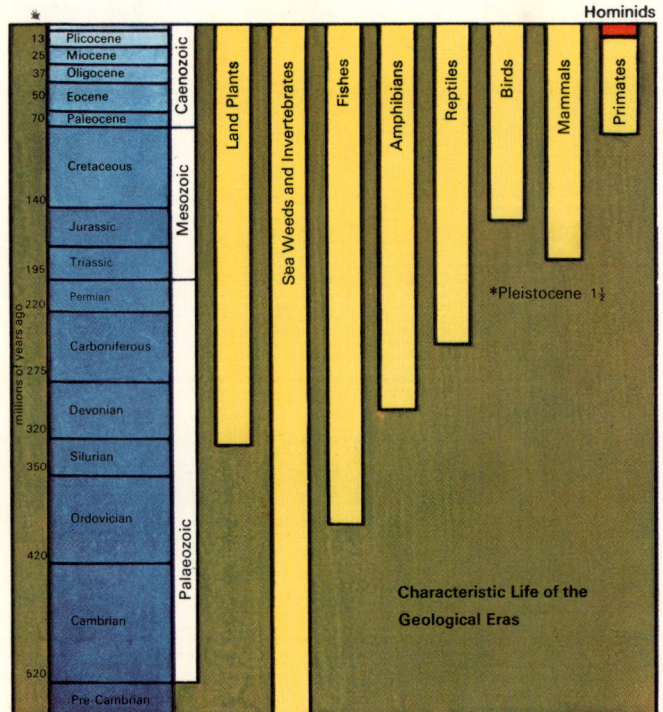

Characteristic Life of the Geological Eras

Above: The upper globe shows the present day distribution of ice in the northern hemisphere, while the lower one shows its maximum extent in Pleistocene times. About 15 million square kilometres of the earth's surface are covered with ice today, but during Pleistocene times it was twice this amount, the ice sheets having moved out from the North and South Poles and down from the mountains of Europe, Asia, America, and New Zealand.

Left: The origin of life is obscure and the subject of much debate. The oldest known forms of life are at least 2,500 million years old. Life gradually evolved from the simple creatures to the complex creatures of today, man being the most advanced. It was not until Ordovician times that there were any animals on earth with backbones – animals which we call vertebrates. Land plants gradually came into being, together with various insects and land animals. The first mammal appeared some 180 million years ago.

After the formation of the earth's crust, it is believed that there gradually came into being an immense land mass, sometimes called Pangea. Gradually this great mass split and drifted to form the continents of today. Such movements have not stopped. They are continuous and progressing.

There can be no doubt that since life appeared on earth, it has gradually evolved, increasing in complexity, as each geological period shows. The highest achievement of this chain of events is man, the first being on earth capable of controlling his surroundings and reasoning out his problems, the product of 2,500 million years of steady evolution.

THE TIME OF MAN

It is really only during the last two million years that man, as we understand him, has developed. The geological term for this time is the Pleistocene Period. (The term Pleistocene means *most recent*.) During this period great ice sheets advanced from the polar lands and high mountain ranges to engulf much of northern Europe, North America, and Asia. Glaciers also advanced in New Zealand.

This period is often called the Great Ice Age, but the ice did not simply advance at this time and then retreat. There were at least four earlier advances of

Above: As the great rivers of ice move down the valleys, they tear pieces of rock from its foundations, grinding and crushing them as they sweep them along. At the glacier's end can be seen a mound of fragments of rock – the *terminal moraine*. If two glaciers join, becoming one, a mass of debris is likely to form in the centre of the glacier, as well as at the sides of the valley. When the glacier retreats, it leaves many reminders of its visit. Valleys which have been glaciated have a cross-section shaped like a "U". Higher in the mountains are semi-circular basins, called cirques, where the glacier originated; many of these are left filled with water.

Right: The Pleistocene Period has been divided according to the various deposits and the fossils found during these times. The deposits naturally reflect the conditions of these spans of time, and the length of time of each section varies.

Pleistocene Glacial (blue) and Interglacial (red) Phases					Climate
Würm	Fourth		Late Wisconsian	Upper Pleistocene	
			Early Wisconsian		
Riss/Würm		Ipswichian	Sangamonian		
Riss	Third		Illinoian		
Mindel/Riss		Hoxnian	Yarmouthian	Middle Pleistocene	
Mindel	Second		Kansanian		
Günz/Mindel		Cromerian	Aftonian		
Günz	First		Nebraskan	Lower Pleistocene	
Alpine Names	Numerical Names	English Names	American Names	Major divisions of the Pleistocene	

Right: River terraces. The advance and retreat of the ice has caused the sea level to vary. Probably a river at one time built up a large mass of mud and silt in its lower reaches and around its mouth. A change in sea level, relative to the land, could cause the river to begin cutting down. and to cut into its own sediments. After a time, only remnants of the former flood plain would be left. A series of changes in sea level would give rise to a number of terraces, as shown in the picture. Such terraces are found along the lower valleys of many rivers throughout the world.

There are many other indications that the sea level has risen since the last of the ice retreated, such as drowned valleys and submerged forests. The great weight of ice on the land during the glacial periods caused it gradually to sink. Since the last ice sheets retreated, however, the land has slowly risen again. Evidence of such rises can be seen in the form of raised beaches, some of which have been found over 270 metres above the present sea level. Such beaches can be found in Scandinavia. Similar rises, though less rapid, are occurring in North America; for example, the old shorelines of the Great Lakes, are now high and dry. In spite of all the water which has been added to the oceans since the ice retreated, sea level is still not as high as it was in pre-Pleistocene times.

0 Post Glacial
1 Third Interglacial
2 Second Interglacial
3 First Interglacial

the ice sheets. The periods of advance of the glaciers and ice sheets are known as glacials, and these are separated by interglacials. It should not be imagined that the ice just moved forward, for it did not. Gradually, over a number of years, the masses of ice moved forward, then possibly retreated a little, only to move on again. The general pattern was to show an advance over a period of many, many years. Even a

Left: A typical scene during glacial times. The changes in climate during the Pleistocene Period had a tremendous effect on the distribution of plants and animals. The picture shows the kinds of animals that would have been found living near the edge of the permanent ice. All of them show certain adaptations to such a harsh life. They would have had to survive extreme cold and be able to obtain a plentiful supply of food when the ground was covered with deep snow. Their coats are thick and woolly — obviously needed to keep warm.

Many of the animals alive today also lived during the ice age, but they are now found in different parts of the world. Shown in the picture are: the mammoth, the bison, the wolf, and the woolly rhinoceros. In the background are reindeer and wild horses. In such an environment, small, stunted trees, much like those which now grow in the far north, would be found.

Right: The scene shows the animals of a typical interglacial. Many such periods of warmth in an otherwise cold period of time were in fact much warmer than our climate today.

Animals such as the hippopotamus are known to have frequented northern Europe and England. Animals shown include the straight-tusked elephant, a rhinoceros, fallow deer, and a lion.

glacial period could be broken by a significantly warmer period called an interstadial.

The Pleistocene is not the only geological period to have suffered an ice age. Other periods affected in this way are the Pre-Cambrian, Cambrian, Late Carboniferous, and possibly the Cretaceous.

The major and minor advances of the ice sheets during Pleistocene times had a tremendous effect on man and his evolution. Because of the complex nature of the deposits, and the difficulty of relating specimens found all over the world with one another, it is not easy to understand the story of man. It is known, for example, that while the ice was advancing in the northern lands, Africa had an increased rainfall. Such periods are called pluvials, and may offer a means of relating the deposits of Europe with Africa.

Man's distribution throughout the world was affected not only by the advances of the ice, but also by changes in sea level. When the sea level was lower than at present, many land-bridges existed. Alaska would have been joined to Asia, Great Britain to Europe, and so on.

Left: Surviving until relatively recent times, at least in North America, the sabre-toothed cat must have been a formidable animal. Many specimens of it have been found in the famous tar pits of Rancho La Brea in Los Angeles. The beast was about the size of the present-day African lion. The very large canine teeth were most likely used for stabbing thick skinned prey such as the contemporary mammoths.

Right: A large elephant-like creature, which survived from earlier times, and eventually died out during the Pleistocene Period. The reason for its very odd tusks is not known. Many other animals did not survive the Pleistocene. These included some massive beasts of South and Central America, such as the giant ground sloths and giant armadillos; a large, wombat-like creature about the size of a rhinoceros; kangaroos up to 3 metres tall; and some giant birds, such as the great auk and the moas.

THE CAUSES OF ICE AGES

Perhaps the most likely cause of ice ages is a variation in the amount of solar radiation received by the earth. Some scientists, however, have argued that the earth's axis has changed, or that the continents have changed position with respect to the pole.

FINDING FOSSIL MAN

The remains of prehistoric man are very rare. Consequently, any modern-day site which may be expected to yield human remains will be excavated with the greatest possible care and attention to detail. Many specialists will be called in to help and give advice. The days of the one-man excavation have long since gone.

One cannot just go out and dig for fossil man. A great deal of careful preparatory work is required. The area will have to be geologically surveyed. It is often the geologist who will first know of likely fossil man localities. Possibly these will be discovered while the area is being geologically mapped.

If a promising deposit is in a very remote area which ordinary maps do not cover, then maps will have to be compiled.

But long before we can go looking for our ancestors, or any other fossil for that matter, parts of these ancient inhabitants of the earth must have been

Right: The animal is being overcome by poisonous gases and dust issuing from the erupting volcano, and will probably collapse into the water in which it is standing. The body will be quickly covered by volcanic dust, and therefore its remains will have an excellent chance of becoming fossilized; in fact, the entire skeleton may remain intact.

Left: An animal has died, and various scavengers are already ripping chunks of flesh from the skeleton. Some of the bones will also be torn away in this manner; what is left behind may be scattered and crushed by animals, the weather, or running water, so that nothing remains for fossilization. Should the pile of bones remaining after the animals have had their feast be covered by silt and mud, there is a good chance of a fossil developing.

preserved. They must have been fossilized. Fossilization is a matter of chance; and it requires even more luck to find the parts when they have been fossilized.

When an animal dies, the flesh will be taken quickly by other animals. Some of the bones will go, too. The remains that are left at the site of death will be subjected to the action of the weather, and perhaps quickly covered. A cloud of volcanic dust can provide instant cover.

The type of soil in which the bones find themselves after death will also decide their state of preservation.

Below: A diagrammatic representation of what happens to bone under different conditions. The type of soil in which a bone is buried after an animal dies is very important if it is to be fossilized:
1. In wet acid soil, the bone is gradually removed and every trace disappears.
2. In wet alkaline soil, fossilization is possible.
3. In dry alkaline soil, a sub-fossil will be formed.
4. In airless and wet conditions, complete preservation will occur. Peat is such a medium.
In Denmark, in peat bogs, specimens of man have been found. These specimens are complete, not merely skeletons, and are about 2,000 years old.

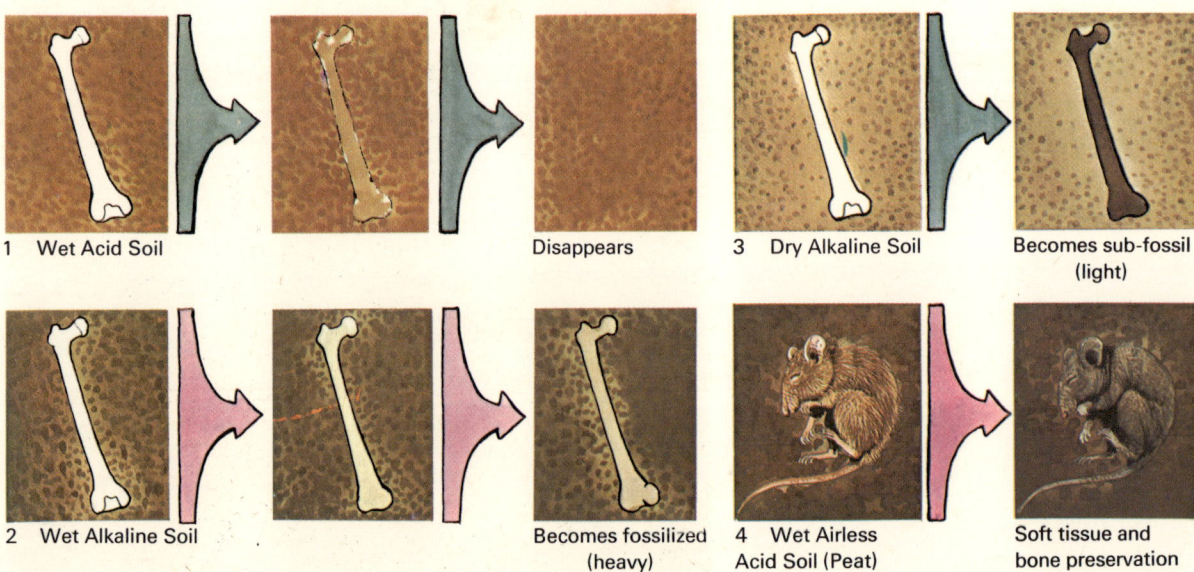

1 Wet Acid Soil → Disappears
3 Dry Alkaline Soil → Becomes sub-fossil (light)
2 Wet Alkaline Soil → Becomes fossilized (heavy)
4 Wet Airless Acid Soil (Peat) → Soft tissue and bone preservation

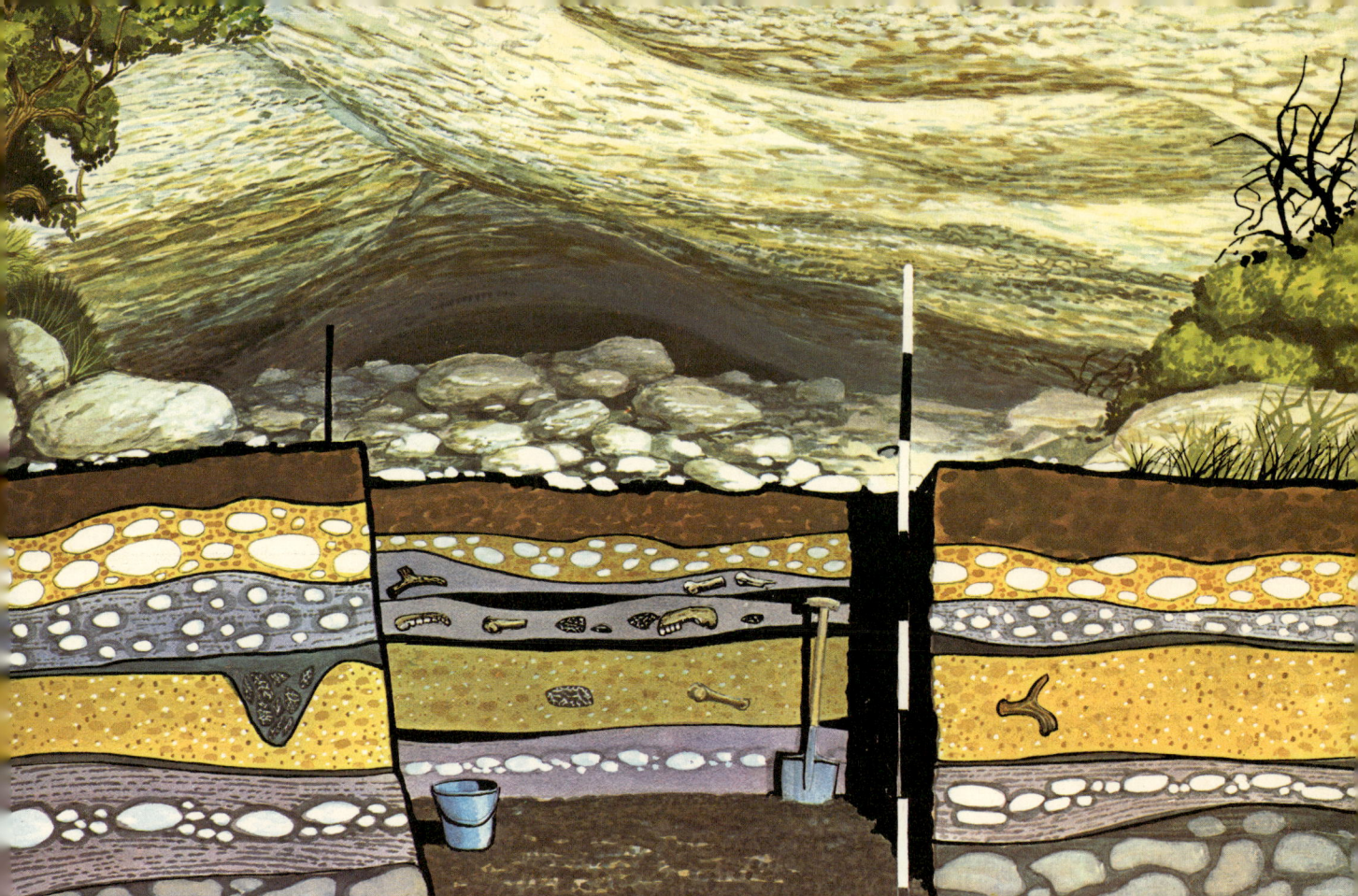

Above: Excavation of a cave site showing the various layers, some of which have evidence of man. Cave deposits are likely places in which to look for fossils.

Caves are often found in regions where limestone is the principal rock type, because rainwater is slightly acid and will dissolve the limestone. The various joints and cracks gradually widen, sometimes forming caves. Under such conditions, what is left in a cave will be buried in an alkaline deposit, a good medium for fossilization.

Many animals made their homes in caves – they lived and died there. Other animals dragged to their cave parts of animals they had killed for food. Early man also used caves for shelter, and eventually began to live in them.

Among the many advantages caves offer, at least to the fossil hunter, one is that bones deposited in such an environment are no longer subjected to the action of the weather.

Rarely is a complete animal found, but when it happens, such discoveries are exciting and useful.

In Siberia, mammoths have been found in the frozen ground. In one famous discovery the beast still had the remains of its last meal in its stomach and grass in its mouth. This particular find is now on display in Leningrad. Its age: 44,000 years! Such finds provide an excellent opportunity to study the diet and skin of these extinct creatures, as well as many other details.

The frozen wastes of Alaska have also provided frozen mammoths. In one case a baby animal was found.

The famous tar pits of Rancho La Brea in California have yielded so many intact skeletons that we have an excellent idea of life as it existed near Los Angeles some 14–15,000 years ago.

From what is now the Ukrainian Soviet Socialist Republic has come a complete woolly rhinoceros,

Top: The development of a fossil bone. Excavation must be done slowly and carefully, the job of cleaning the remains in the laboratory is a long and laborious process.

Above: Computers have helped greatly in the study of the remains of prehistoric man. They enable scientists to make extensive statistical calculations far more quickly than before. Fossil specimens can now be grouped by using the technique of multivariate analysis. Also, it is possible to calculate the approximate distance between such groups.

preserved in salt and oil. Again, it has been possible to examine anatomical details of this animal which would normally be lost forever.

Such rare finds enable us to know a great deal more about the animals that lived at a crucial time in man's development.

Caves have been mentioned as a likely source for bones. Another place is in deposits which have had their origins in lakes.

The shore of a lake, a very likely site of prehistoric man, would also have an accumulation of bones, representing "leftovers" of the various meals – and possibly even of the men themselves.

Traces of tools might also remain. When the level of a lake rises, and men retreat, the former camp is covered by water and sediment.

Gradually the bones are fossilized. Perhaps at a later date, with changes in climate and geological structure, the layers laid down in the lake will be exposed as the rock in a valley wall. Hence, such a place is generally considered to be a good "hunting ground" for specimens of fossil man.

If a site is to be excavated, it will be done carefully and deliberately. The exact position and distribution of all fragments will be recorded along with their indicated relationships. The whole operation will also be photographed so that pictures may be reproduced in any publication about the excavation.

Trained laboratory technicians must also preserve the bones as they are discovered to prevent them from deteriorating or drying out. The bones may also have to be strengthened to withstand shipment to the museum or university.

Once received at the laboratory, careful unpacking is necessary. Attempts are made to release the specimens from the rock in which they were discovered. Broken parts are repaired and casts made for further study.

The production of casts is important not only for additional study at the institute where the specimen itself is, but also for transmission to other places. Scientists throughout the world are able to compare various finds without risking the original specimens at all.

From any given site bones may be found which will not necessarily belong to the same kind of animal.

Above: Excavation of an important site in progress. The dig has been operating for some time, as indicated by the large amount of earth that has been removed. Because it is necessary to do this with great care, it has been a very tedious task. Each time a specimen is unearthed, it is left in place on its own hill of soil.

Different specimens have been found at different levels. The relationship of all these specimens to each other is of vital importance.

Before some of the more fragile items can be removed from the site, they must be strengthened. One of the specimens has already been treated. The two men are busy working on another. The specimens are wrapped in wet tissue and encased in plaster of Paris.

Considerable care is taken in such excavations to gather every possible piece of information. The one piece lost could be the most important item.

The entire site is photographed at its various stages of excavation.

Indeed, it is unlikely that they will all be of the same one. From such a confusion of broken pieces, palaeontologists (the scientists who study fossils) must try to sort out and classify them.

Several factors can help. Most of the higher animals are bilaterally symmetrical (i.e. the same structurally, on both sides). Thus, missing parts can often be restored by reference to, and the copying of the opposite side.

From first examination, a trained eye will quickly sort out the main types of animal bones. Fossil hunters are aware of the anatomical features of these animals and therefore know what to look for if they get a certain part of the skeleton.

Once the bones of an animal are sorted out, it is often possible to identify its age and sex.

Any species may have great variation of form. (Think of how men differ!) The range of size is significant in dealing with the remains of fossil man, and until the advent of computers it was possible to make only simple statistical calculations. Now extensive calculations can be made in seconds.

Above: Great skill is required to cast fossil bones. Many materials are used today – plaster of Paris, various plastics, fibreglass.
  Casting must be done carefully, in order to reproduce the various features accurately and preserve the original specimen.

Right: A scientist puts together the pieces of a skull which have been recovered from an excavation. Any such reconstruction is a tedious job. Each fragment must be carefully studied before it can be positioned.

DATING THE FINDS

The science of dating is called geochronology. Two types of dating are used: relative dating and absolute dating.

Relative dating, as the name suggests, is arrived at by comparing a find against a known series. It does not reveal the precise age of an object. If, for example, tools are found in a dig, these will almost certainly have a characteristic shape, manufactured in a way which is recognizable. By referring to a known sequence of tools, it is possible to obtain a relative date.

Other techniques used in relative dating are stratigraphy, pollen analysis and fluorine analysis.

The geologist works by assuming the law of superposition. This means that any given stratum of rock is older than the one above it and younger than the one below it.

By detailed analysis of pollen found in various deposits it is possible to build up a picture of the changes in vegetation over a long period. From such studies much can be learned of past climate, which is particularly useful in covering the period of man, the Pleistocene, which has seen many variations in climate all over the world.

The type of botanist who studies pollen and spores of plants is called a palynologist.

The technique of fluorine analysis makes it possible to determine whether or not bones found in a deposit have all been there for the same period of time.

It is not used for absolute dating because the way bones take up fluorine depends on the fluorine content of the ground water. It therefore varies from place to place.

Fluorine testing is most useful in determining whether or not a hoax or fraud is being attempted.

Nitrogen content of buried bones tends to diminish with age. Hence, this is another method of determining whether or not all the bones from a particular deposit are the same age.

ABSOLUTE DATING

Absolute dating gives somewhat more dramatic results, which are not necessarily the most important. It is, however, very impressive to be able to say that a particular bone is a specific number of million years old. Age fascinates people.

From a different site

From one site

Above: An early method of absolute dating called *varve analysis*. Originally used in Sweden to gauge the time elapsed since the passing of the ice, it relied on the simple fact that the lake deposits of this region are distinctive. The fast-running streams of summer bring down great quantities of coarse material. In winter, much of the ground is frozen, and only the finest particles find their way into the lake. Alternating layers of coarse and fine sediment result. In a section of such a deposit it is possible to count the varves to ascertain the age.

Left: Over the years, by means of hundreds of examples, archaeologists have come to know the sequence of man's tools. Thus, if certain tools are found along with some bones, it is possible to give a relative date to this site.

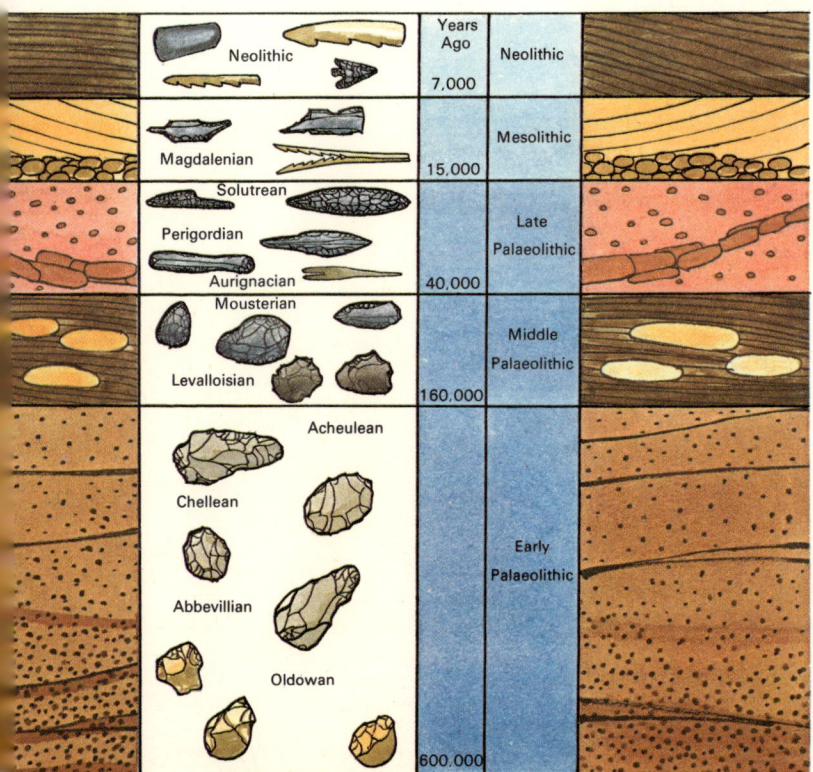

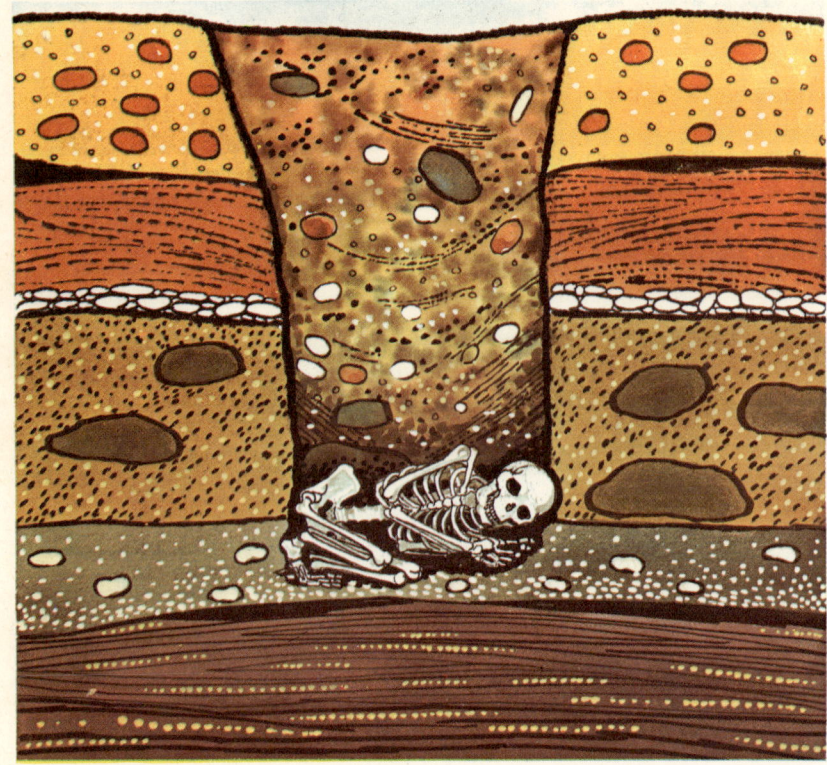

Left: Burials such as the one shown in the picture can supply a false idea of age.
  It is important that such points are considered during excavation, because once the soil and rock have been removed, it is too late.

It is therefore apparent that the function of absolute dating is to reveal how old an object is in terms of years.

Again, many methods have been used to calculate this. An early and rather novel method is that of varve analysis. Another is to count the growth rings of trees. This science is called dendrochronology.

RADIOACTIVE DATING

Perhaps the most famous method of radioactive dating is known as the radiocarbon method. This utilizes the fact that radioactive carbon (C^{14}) is present in the atmosphere as carbon dioxide, and becomes absorbed into plants and eventually into an animal's tissues as the animal eats the plants throughout its life. When the animal dies, the radioactivity of the remains declines at a known rate, until half of the C^{14} is left after 5,730 years. (This period is called the half-life of C^{14}.) Geiger counters are used to measure how much C^{14} is left in the remains of the animal, and knowing this and the decay rate, the age of the remains can be easily calculated.

Left: A sample placed in a heating tube is converted into carbon dioxide.

Below: A Geiger counter measures the residual radioactivity present in a specimen.

Radiocarbon dating, one of the most efficient forms of dating, was first used in 1959.

It is possible to use this method to determine the age of a specimen as old as 70,000 years. When dating material older than 40,000 years, however, special equipment is also needed.

Tree Ring Counting

recent tree

ancient tree

Above: Example of tree ring counting, or *dendrochronology*, another way of obtaining an absolute date.

The record preserved in the annual growth rings of a tree can show not only its age, but sometimes can indicate past climatic conditions. This method of dating has its limitations, and datable material is in short supply.

Most people who have visited a large museum have seen cross-sections of giant trees. Important dates in history are often painted on the rings.

POTASSIUM-ARGON DATING

Another useful method of dating, which has provided reliable dates, is that known as the potassium-argon technique.

Potassium which occurs naturally, is known to contain an isotope called potassium-40. This decays, as in the case of carbon, into a gas called argon. The potassium-argon method is rarely used to date deposits less than 20,000 years old, since its half-life is about 1,350 million years.

Volcanic deposits generally yield material which is suitable for such analysis, and this has proved most useful in the case of the dating of the rocks of Olduvai Gorge in East Africa, an important site for fossil man discoveries.

NEWER METHODS OF DATING

Of late, a new method of dating based on uranium has been developed. It is particularly useful for dating cores of silt from a sea bed.

Much care is needed to obtain reliable results by means of radioactive dating. In the past there have been many inconsistencies, and some incorrectly dated rocks have caused a great deal of difficulty in interpreting finds. So far, the potassium-argon method seems to have provided the most consistent results.

It is certain that dating methods and techniques will be greatly improved in the future and that the results already achieved have been of considerable value.

The finding of fossil man is fraught with complications. Even when a suitable site is found it is difficult to extract the specimens and interpret them.

Deposits throughout the world have to be correlated, and to this end various dating techniques have been universally established. The fauna and flora contemporary with man must be understood if we are to know anything of the land in which he lived.

The Pleistocene was a period of great climatic changes. But through diligent work, men have gradually established the age of the various major events of this period of man.

MAJOR OLD WORLD DIVISIONS OF THE PLEISTOCENE AND HOLOCENE PERIOD IN YEARS BP

(BEFORE THE PRESENT)

Holocene
Recent Post Glacial   10,000

Upper Pleistocene
Würm Glaciation
Riss-Würm Interglacial   100,000
Riss Glaciation

Middle Pleistocene
Mindel-Riss Interglacial
Mindel Glaciation   450,000
Günz-Mindel Interglacial

Lower Pleistocene
Villafranchian
Günz Glaciation   1,000,000
Pre-Günz stages

Boundary between Pliocene and Pleistocene
    2–3,000,000 years BP

Left: In recent years, our understanding of the ocean and its floor has greatly increased. Useful knowledge of past climates is obtained by studying the fossil content of cores of silt brought up from various parts of the ocean floor. There is still much research to be done in this field.

Core sample from a deep sea bore.

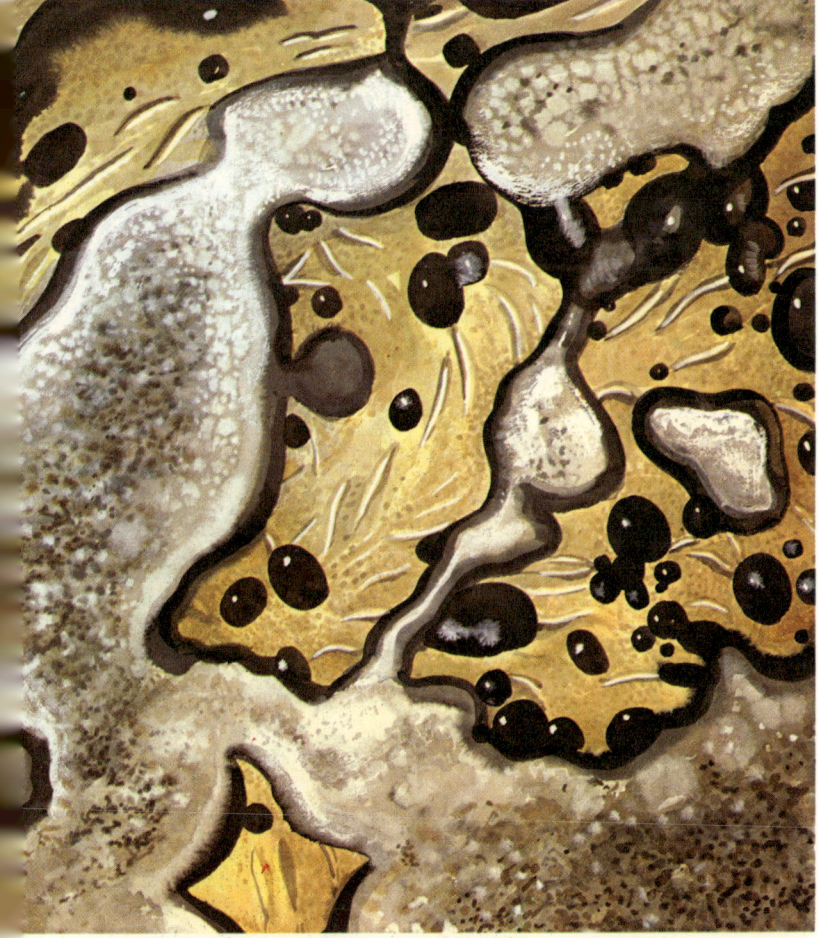

Left: Fission tracks in obsidian. The study of fission tracks is one of the newest developments in absolute dating techniques.

One of the results of volcanic activity is the formation of a glassy mineral called obsidian. Like some man-made glass, it breaks into curved pieces with razor-sharp edges. Early man used to make pieces of this natural glass into cutting tools.

This ancient glass is contaminated by the radioactive element uranium. Radioactive material decays with time, by splitting up (fission). The minute particles that "explode off" when fission occurs leave fission tracks. These tracks show up under a microscope, if the sample is etched with certain acids (rather like secret writing).

We know how long a piece of glass containing a certain amount of uranium would take to become non-radioactive. That is, we know the length of its radioactive life. But by irradiating it (bombarding it with X-rays) all the remaining atoms capable of fission can be exploded immediately. We can find out how near the end of its life a specimen is by counting the number of fission tracks already in it, then hastening its "death" by irradiating it, and then recounting the number of tracks. The difference in the number of tracks indicates how much longer that specimen would have been naturally radioactive, and hence how old it was at the time it was first examined.

THE FRAMEWORK OF MAN

"The present is the key to the past" is a famous geological quotation. In attempting to study prehistoric man and the evolutionary lines which lead to modern man, it is necessary to understand the structure of modern man.

The shape and arrangement of bones are important, and must be considered in relation to the way man lives and acts.

Besides man himself, it is also necessary to understand the makeup of other primates. But it should be remembered that in studying a living primate, or for that matter any living plant or animal, what is being examined is the present end product of a particular evolutionary line.

To find out when these different forms arose, we shall have to look at the fossil record. Apes are not closely related to man in the sense that man came from the apes. The division of the two lines of development took place long ago. By studying present day forms, however, and comparing their structure and mode of life, it is possible to interpret, at least in part, the many fossil remains of primates which have been discovered.

Man is a vertebrate, and as such possesses a typical skeleton, which has a number of functions. It provides anchorage for many muscles. All body tissues are supported by the skeleton. Finally, it gives protection. The various important organs found in the chest are suitably protected by the rib cage. The all-important brain is tucked inside a good, solid shell of bone.

What is this framework made of? The answer:

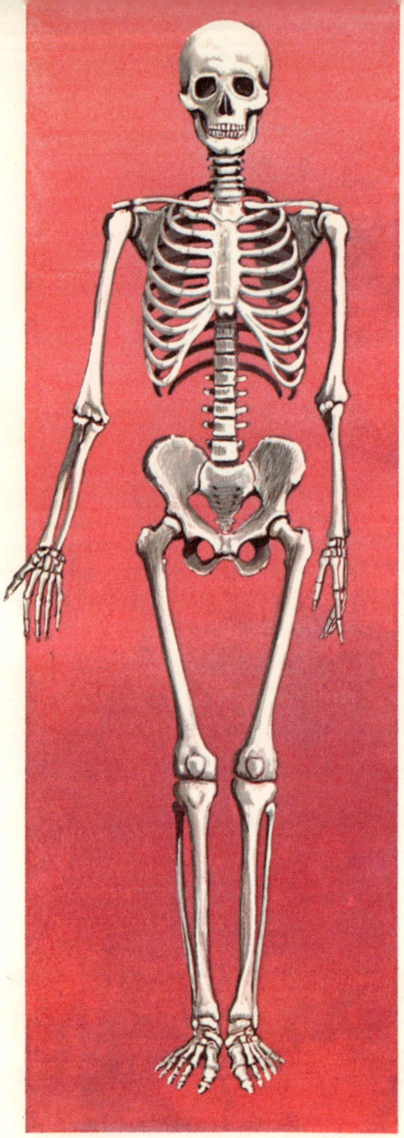

Above: The skeleton of a man contains 206 bones, although it is not easy to distinguish all of them. The skeleton is divided into two parts: the axial skeleton, which includes the backbone (vertebral column), the rib cage, and the skull; and the appendicular skeleton, comprised of the limbs and limb girdles.

Right: Bone which has been burned will lose organic matter. All material that remains is inorganic, and will be extremely brittle.

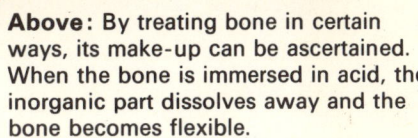

Above: By treating bone in certain ways, its make-up can be ascertained. When the bone is immersed in acid, the inorganic part dissolves away and the bone becomes flexible.

bone. When we discover the remains of prehistoric man, it is his bones we find, and very often his teeth. The teeth are the hardest part of the skeleton.

Rarely are any soft parts preserved, so it may seem incredible that so much is known about fossil animals.

Bone would not seem to be of much use in interpreting what our ancestors looked like, however the assumption is wrong. The size of the bones provides a reasonable estimate of the size of the original person. As will be seen by the study of modern man and by comparisons with other living primates, bones can disclose much information about the evolution of man.

There are canals, or passages, in bones that once contained nerves and blood vessels. Grooves and impressions reveal where muscles have been. Careful interpretation of such structures is necessary because of the variations possible within any single species of animal. For example, there may be two passages in a certain bone of one specimen, whereas in another specimen only one passage (serving the same purpose) will be found in a similar bone.

Bones may also reveal poor diet, disease and injury. Such disclosures are not too common, but they are known. The study of ancient disease, palaeopathology, has advanced greatly in recent years.

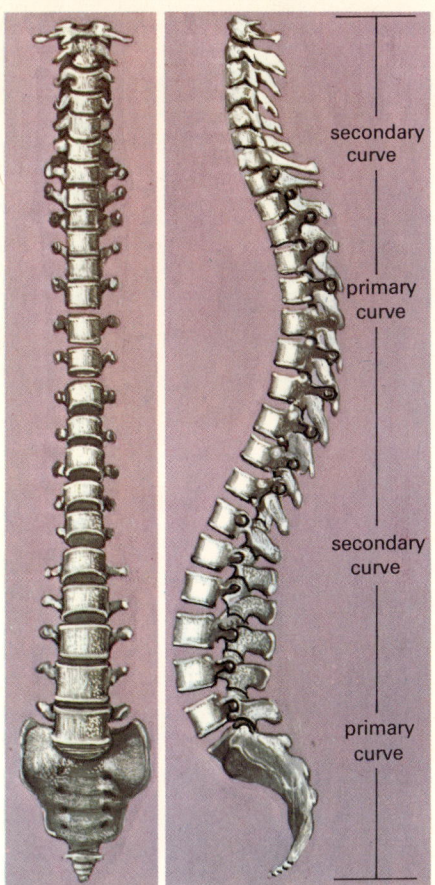

Above: The vertebral column, or backbone, is made up of small blocks of bone with discs between them. These discs help reduce friction and cushion jarring movements. The individual blocks or vertebrae, increase in size from the head downward and become smaller again at the base of the spine.

The backbone is often thought to be straight, but this is not so. If it were straight, man would not be able to keep his head in an upright position.

Because of the various curves of the vertebral column, the head is held in perfect balance on top of its "pole", and therefore the human body is beautifully aligned.

Left: Bone is alive, for it contains living cells that must have oxygen and food. The difference between bone and muscle for example is that the bone's living cells are encased in a hard matrix.

A microscope is needed to reveal the structure of bone, and the picture shows, (far left), a cross-section, and (near left), a longitudinal section.

The large holes seen in the cross-section, called *haversian canals*, house the blood vessels.

Around these are the bone cells occupying spaces called *lacunae*. Fine channels connect the lacunae and the canals.

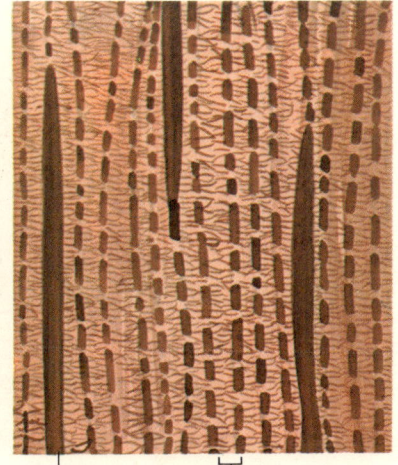

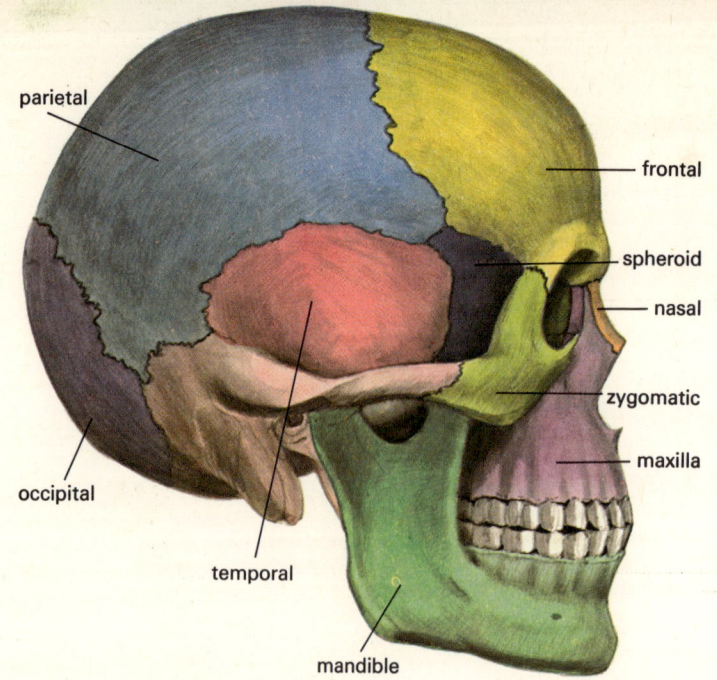

Left: The skull of man is a complex structure consisting of twenty bones. The part which protects the brain is known as the *cranium*, and is made up of eight bones. The pieces are joined together along an irregular line called the *suture*. This produces a rigid "box".

At the very base of the skull lies the *occipital*, a bone in which there is a large hole. Through it passes the spinal cord on its way from the brain to the backbone. It is the position of this large hole, called the *foramen magnum*, which used to determine whether an animal can maintain an upright position.

The upper jaw, which also helps to form part of the eye orbit, consists of two *maxillary* bones; the lower jawbone is called the *mandible*, and is the only bone in the skull which moves.

THE BODY OF MAN

Man has certain characteristics which set him aside from the other primates. If we are to interpret the remains of early man, it is important to see and understand how these differences appear in the skeleton of modern man.

Man walks upright, his teeth are different from those of the apes, and his brain is well-developed. The brain is enclosed in a rigid box which is high and has a rounded vault. There is sufficient space for muscles to operate the jaw. The skull of the gorilla, by contrast, is topped by a crest in the middle to give further support to the jaw muscles. The gorilla's skull is not balanced as man's is, and almost all of its weight lies in front. To compensate for this, the gorilla has very large neck muscles.

The face of man developed as it did because of the arrangement of the teeth – it is a direct result of the dentition. The face is relatively flat, and set below the cranium, the chin well-developed. Unlike many of our ancestors, the ridges of the eyes, or brow ridges, effect only very slight bumps on the forehead. There is a prominent nose, but not a snout, due to the fact that in man the sense of smell has become less important, in contrast to other primates. Another characteristic of our early living is forward-looking eyes. Many animals – for example dogs, cats, and horses – have eyes which look to the side.

The skeletal reasons for our appearance are now clear. The massive brow ridges of our ancestors and the shape of the skull are features which help to separate the ancient and the modern.

Below: The technical names given to the different views of the skull. The *frontal* view, looking toward the face; the *basal*, looking upward from the floor; the *occipital*, the backview; the *vertical*, from directly above.

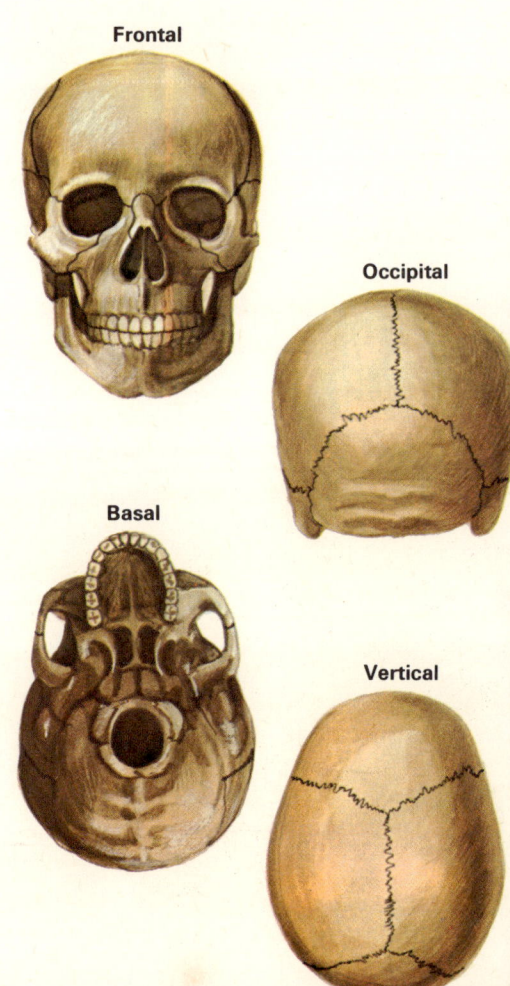

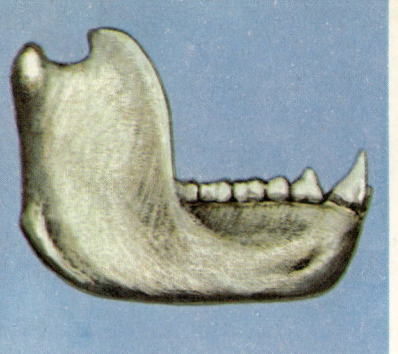
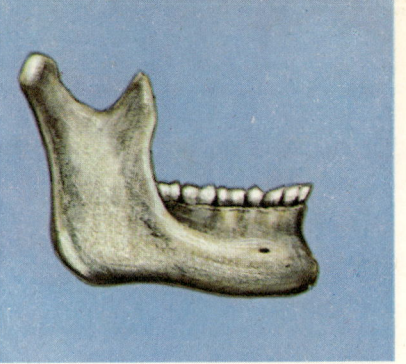

Left: Diagram showing the differences between ape and human jaws.

Below: Pictures of actual jaws of ape (above) and man (below). Human canine teeth are much smaller than those of the ape. The so-called dental arcade of the apes is rectangular, while that of man is more U shaped, or parabolic.

These features are very important when dealing with fossil finds, and are vital in assigning remains to a correct group.

The upper jaw is made up of paired maxillae. They fit together to form the roof of the mouth and the floor of the nasal passages.

The teeth fit into sockets in both the upper and lower jaws.

The part of the tooth above the surface is called the crown. The surface on which biting takes place is the occlusal surface.

Human beings grow two sets of teeth during their lifetime. The first set, the milk teeth, number 20 and the full adult set, 32.

The teeth of modern man are as characteristic as his jaw. In male apes especially, the canines are longer than the rest of the teeth. They are the fangs. The very front teeth, the incisors, are relatively small. In the pre-molars and molars, there are also differences between apes and man.

Many suppositions have been set forth to account for this change in the pattern of the teeth. A true determination is made difficult by the fact that only the male ape possesses long canines – not the female. As both eat the same type of food, diet alone cannot account for it. Perhaps it has to do with displays of aggression.

Some of the theories advanced are: changes in hormones, the gradual incorporation of the canine teeth into a complex of front teeth used in biting, and the advent of tool manufacture.

The idea of a complex of biting teeth seems reasonable, but the matter is undoubtedly much more complicated, and the truth probably draws something from each theory.

It could be that behaviour plays a part, the canines being reduced so as to avoid conflict in the group.

Teeth of different animals tend to reflect different diets and therefore different ways of life.

Much has been written of the earliest men. These australopithecines, as they are called, have been divided into two main groups partly because of their teeth. One group represents a more robust vegetable-eating form and the other a smaller form (generally called the gracile australopithecine) believed to have had a mixed diet of vegetables and meat. There are many other differences between these two early men, as we shall see.

Teeth are therefore important, as they tell us much about their owner. As we have noted, because of their hardness, teeth also represent the most prevalent remains of prehistoric man.

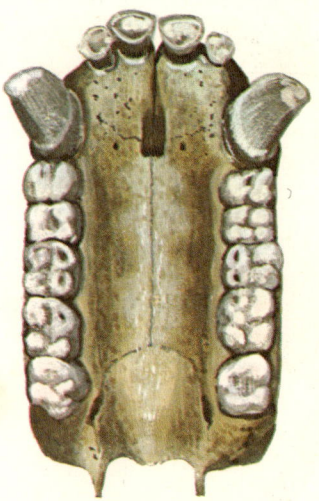
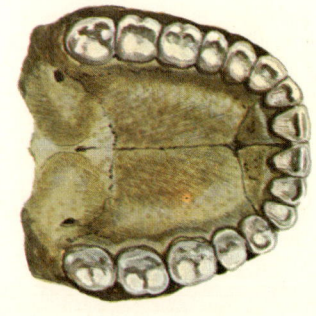

One of man's most important characteristics is the way he moves about. He walks upright on two legs, a method of locomotion called bipedalism.

Why certain primates came to adopt a life on the ground instead of in the trees is the subject of many theories. The ground was not likely to be an easy place for mobility or survival, since the first primates would not be as agile as man – nor would they have the advantage of his brain capacity.

Of course, a group of apes did not suddenly find itself living on the ground. This descent from the trees was a gradual process.

It is now known that other members of the primate group spend some time on the ground, attempting to walk upright. In the main they succeed, and the incentive for their attempts is usually food. They have been observed collecting food and carrying it to a more suitable place to eat it.

Below left: The soccer player demonstrates the lower limb in action. The upper part of the limb consists of a large bone, the *femur*, and the lower part is made up of two bones, the *tibia* and the smaller *fibula*.

Below: The bones of the foot are relatively small. Those of the ankle region are called the *tarsals*. Towards the toes are the *metatarsals* and the *phalanges*. The upper illustration shows the medial arch of the human foot, a foot which, unlike the ape's, lies flat on the ground and is unable to grasp. The big toe receives most of the force as the foot pushes off at the beginning of a step. By examining the toe bones, we can understand why man walks the way he does.

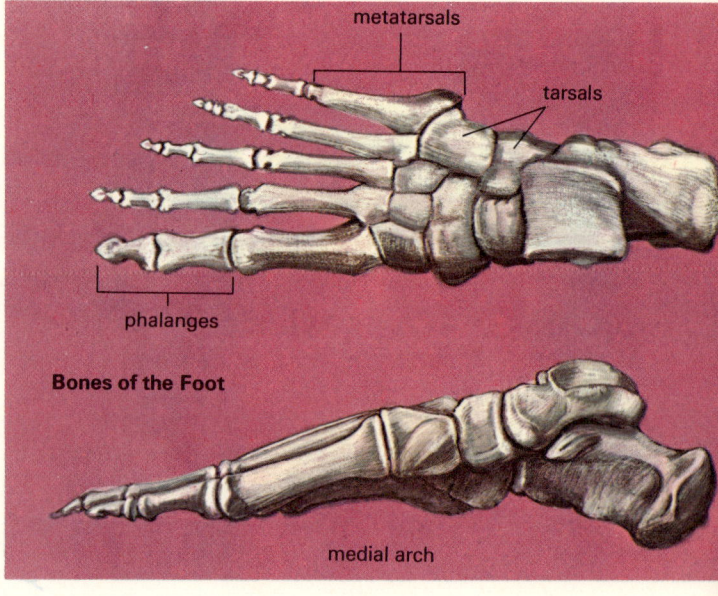

Bones of the Foot

It could well be that man's remote ancestors found it useful to have the forelimbs, the hands, free to carry things – not only food, but also their young. A change in diet from vegetables to meat might also have been the explanation. Hunters need to travel long distances, particularly if they are not armed with very advanced weapons, in order to kill their prey. Also, after a successful kill, there would be more meat than one person could eat, so the food could be shared. It would therefore have to be brought back to the temporary home.

The element of defence cannot be ruled out in seeking explanations for the upright stance, since it

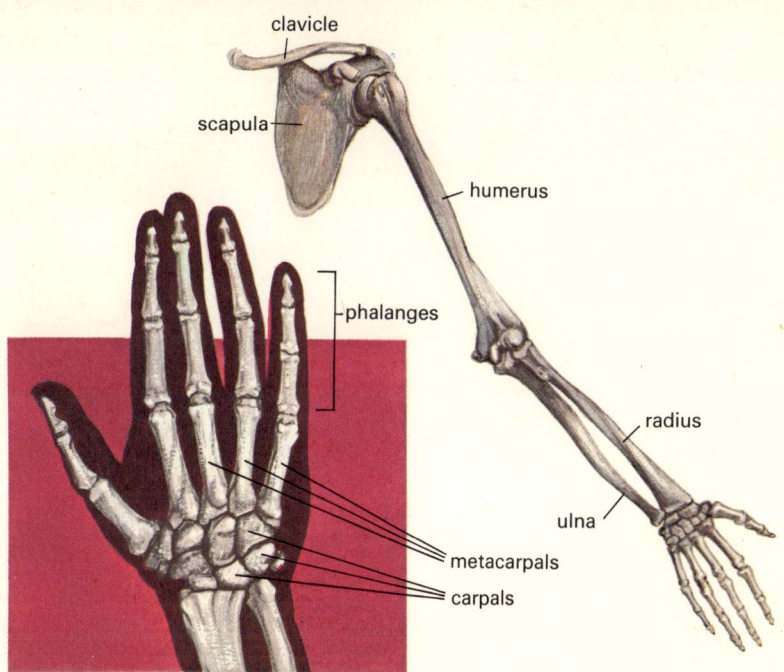

Right: The bones of the hand are not unlike those of the foot. The three main hand bones are those in the wrist, the *carpals*. These connect to the *metacarpals* and the *phalanges*.

The arm, like the leg, has a single large bone at the top, and two smaller bones below.

The actual shoulder girdle is made up of the *scapula* and *clavicle*, better known as the shoulder blade and collarbone.

Below: The arm has a wide range of movement, in contrast to the more limited movements of the leg. Such movements, and the bone structures that make them possible, are primitive reminders of man's tree-living origins.

The hand, too, is a simple structure, except for the thumb, which is able to make more intricate movements, as, for example, when it comes into direct contact with the fingertips.

would make an animal appear to be much larger, and possibly deter an opponent's attack. The advantage of having a wider field of view when standing upright is another possible reason for assuming such a position.

Undoubtedly, justifications for man's stance are many. The changing environment at this crucial time in man's evolution may have been a major reason. The great forests of the earlier part of the Caenozoic were gradually receding, and new environments were being created, areas where foliage would not be as dense. In any case, it is conceivable that these primates lived at the edge of forest areas and gradually made their way towards the grassy plain.

The use of tools is also equated with man's upright stance. Some authorities believe that man first learned to use tools and *then* turned to bipedalism, so that he could have his hands free for such use.

Man's skeleton naturally shows much evidence of man's method of walking. If the right bone is found at a prehistoric site, it is possible to conclude from this whether or not its owner walked upright, and also whether or not the walk was similar to our own.

There is a large hole in the base of the skull called the foramen magnum. Its specific location will indicate an upright stance. In man, this hole is set well forward and opens downwards. In the apes – for example the gorillas – it is set further back and the opening is directed backward rather than downward.

A significant feature of all the bones of the skull is their light weight.

Right: The two basic grips that man uses are shown here. The use of the hands has greatly developed since man first began walking erect.

It has been proved that man's early tools could have been operated using only the power grip. It was only later, apparently, that the precision technique came into use, as primitive man's brain became more developed.

The precision grip was undoubtedly used in later versions of hand-axes and finely-shaped flints.

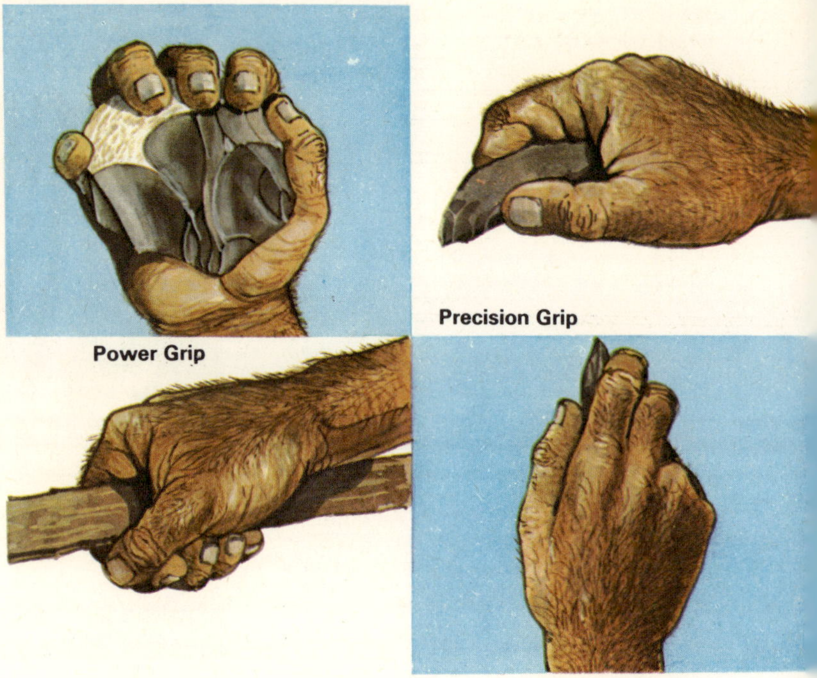

Power Grip

Precision Grip

Another feature of man is his spine, and of particular interest is the forward curve in the region of the pelvis and lower back. The blocks, or vertebrae, which make up this portion of the spine, are wedge-shaped. They are taller at the front than at the back. The discs between them show a similar pattern.

It is the spinal curves that allow the head to balance so well on top. It is held perfectly, unlike the ape's, which we have mentioned.

Another feature centres on the pelvis. Human hips have a definite shape which allows the upright position to be maintained; the gorilla is unable to stand up straight because of a large and very long pelvis. Gradually man's hip blades have become smaller, and the shape has become somewhat like that of a basket.

Below: This picture illustrates the two different grips as employed by modern man. The power grip used on the hammer depends on the inside of the hand for strength, and allows great power to be applied by impact to the head of the nail.

The grip demonstrated by the hand holding the pencil, though not as strong, allows for more precision.

Many delicate movements are involved in writing and drawing.

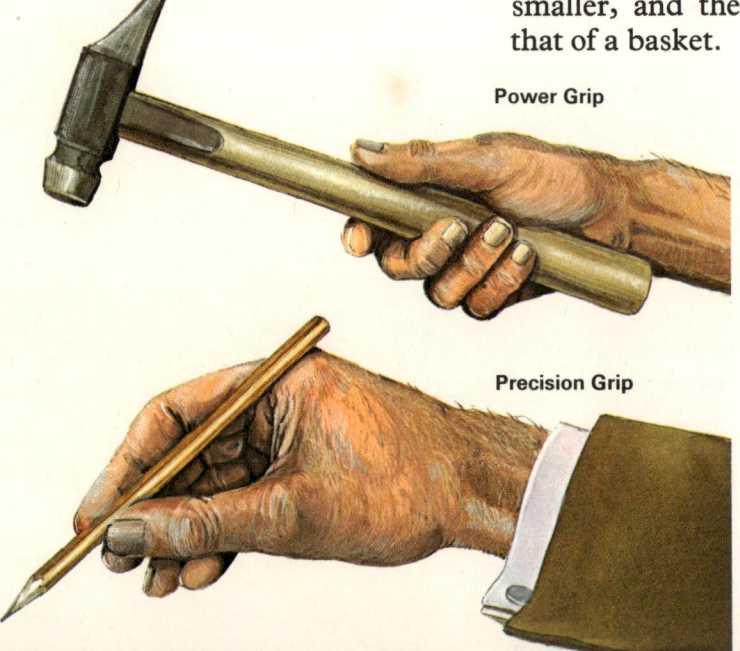

Power Grip

Precision Grip

This "basket" holds the various organs. The weight of the body is held directly above and the centre of gravity falls within the base.

The hip socket is large, as is the head of the bone in the upper leg. This helps absorb the shocks of movement, and provides anchorage for the powerful muscles needed to propel man forward.

Thus there are a number of features in the hips which are useful in interpreting fossil material. Conclusions are possible on the method of locomotion and the ability to stand completely upright.

Man's method of locomotion is also shown in his feet, which are very different from those of the apes.

The foot is really a spring under tension. Because of the way in which body weight is transmitted along and across the foot as we move, certain bones have developed characteristics which can help in reconstructing the story of man.

As man walks, the weight passes down the outside of the foot and across to the big toe, which gives the final push off the ground as he moves forward. The bones which disclose this method of moving are certain of the metatarsals, which are more robust than usual, and also the end part of the big toe.

It was this knowledge which led a very prominent physical anthropologist to what might seem an impossible conclusion. A big toe bone found in Olduvai Gorge, Tanzania, was, on its own, so distinctive that it was possible to conclude that its owner could have walked as we do. He was able to stride along, not just go along in short steps or jog along. The age of this find is put at about one million years.

The upper limb girdle which allows so much freedom is really a carry-over from man's past, or more accurately, from man's ancestors. It had its origin during the time of life in the trees, where swinging from branch to branch was the most practical means of locomotion.

The hand is simple and the only change is that the thumb can be brought into contact with the tops of the fingers, allowing a good grip. It is this feature which allows man to perform so many manual functions.

To achieve intricate and co-ordinated movements requires control, and a more highly developed brain than the early ancestors would have had.

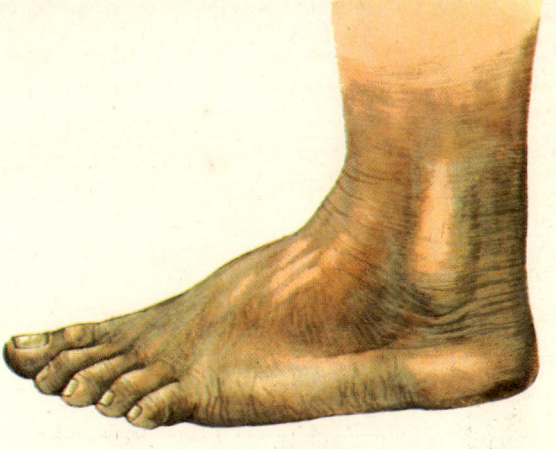

Above: The human foot is a remarkable piece of engineering. It has two basic jobs to perform: it must pass the weight of the body on to the ground, and it must transmit the forces which enable man to walk.

A highly specialized piece of equipment, the foot has a sole that lies almost flat on the floor, and a big toe that is set with the rest of the toes.

It is impossible to grasp with the human foot, though this was not always the case.

The toes are relatively short. There are two arches in every foot, which run from front to back and from side to side.

The foot, though vitally important to man, is probably one of the most ignored parts of the body. But anyone who has had even the most minor foot ailment, such as an ingrowing toenail, knows that it renders walking nearly impossible.

Below: An ape's foot. Not only is it hairier than the human foot shown above, but the toes are longer. The large toe is set apart from the rest, and it does not lie flat on the ground.

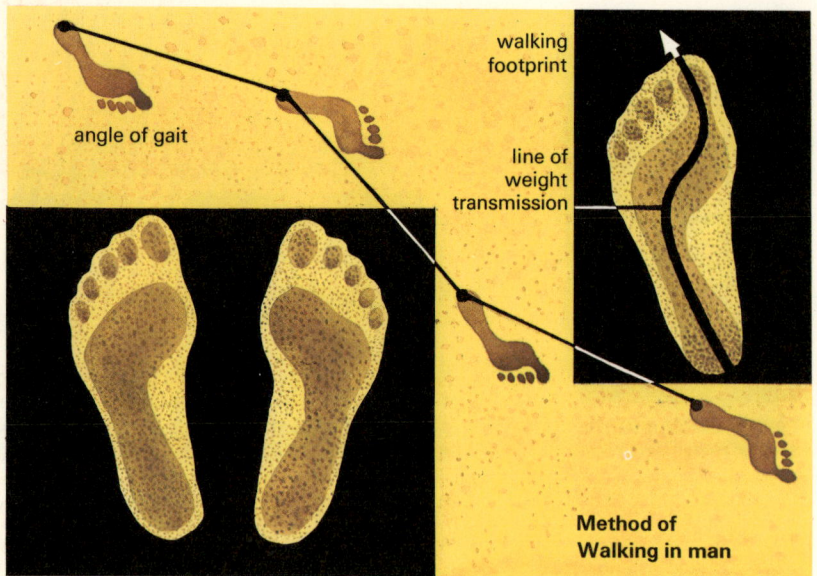

Left: Mobility is an essential function of man. This is made possible by his ability to walk. Walking is really a controlled form of falling. More difficult than it looks, it requires tremendous co-ordination, control, and balance of muscular power in the back, hips, legs, and feet.

As a man puts out one foot to walk, his centre of gravity moves forward. He begins to "fall" forward, only to recover his balance before his foot reaches the ground.

If we were to draw a line along the ground to represent the movement of an individual's centre of gravity during walking, it would be depicted as a zigzag course, as shown in the diagram.

Transmission of weight on the foot also takes place, travelling along the outside and then across to the big toe.

The hand is simple because we have retained the original five digits. Some animals, for example horses and cows, have modified this basic arrangement. The original number of fingers and toes has been reduced.

MAN'S MOST PRIZED POSSESSION

Man's brain is his most valuable asset. Writers refer to its great size and its tremendous capabilities, which cannot be denied. It is indeed a remarkable instrument of the body.

Man owes his place as the most advanced member of the animal kingdom to his brain.

The brain is required to interpret hundreds and thousands of messages coming to it from many sources. Nerves in the skin, muscles and joints feed it with information. The sense organs – the eyes, ears, nose, and tongue – also provide it with messages.

It receives all these, identifies them, and interprets them. More than that, it sets in motion suitable responses to them all, and determines how quickly all of this is to be done.

It is also the home of our emotions, our personality, and our memory. Just think of the number of items the brain must remember – and it is not merely remembering but also knowing what to do about them. For example: recognizing a knife, fork and spoon; recognizing a car and getting out of its way if it is heading straight toward you; knowing where you live, and where things are in your house. The brain must also absorb the information you may get in a schoolroom or from books.

Below: Assuming that we correctly identify the parts of a skeleton's remains, and that they are fairly complete, it is possible to determine the sex of the individual who has been unearthed. To do this with certainty, we must have the pelvis. The pelvis in the lower picture is that of a male; the one on the top, that of a female. The female pelvis is broader and flatter than the male pelvis. The pelvic cavity in the female is also larger, to accommodate the birth of a baby.

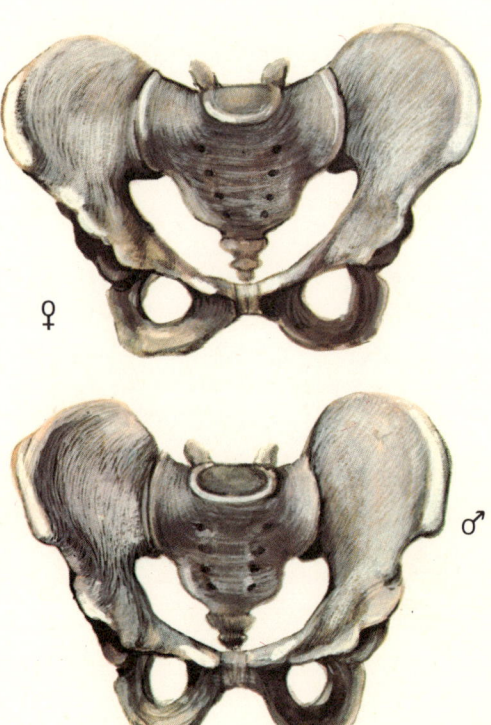

Man's brain, however, is not the largest in the world, and even among men the size ranges from 1,000 to 2,000 c.c. Elephants and whales have larger brains, as we may imagine.

Since these animals are less intelligent than man, it cannot be brain size alone which gives man his advantage.

It must be recognized, however, that the larger the brain, the more cells there are, and therefore more message links are possible.

Perhaps most important is the relationship of brain size to the total size of the animal. Elephants and whales, of course, are among the larger examples.

There is no convincing link between intelligence and brain size. The way in which the connections are made in the brain cells, and the number of such connections, must be significant factors.

One can only speculate about the evolution of the brain. We may be aware of increased size from the remains of skulls, but what of intelligence? The various tools left by prehistoric man are, so far, the only help in understanding this phenomenon.

The behaviour of prehistoric man is, for the most part, lost. By studying living forms in their natural surroundings, however, we are gradually learning how behaviour patterns could have developed.

Despite the advances of recent research, it is possible that we shall never know the entire story; we are, in fact, still a long way from proving man's evolution from the other primates. We can expect to find physical remains which will confirm or shatter evolutionary theories – but with the brain, much will continue to be speculation.

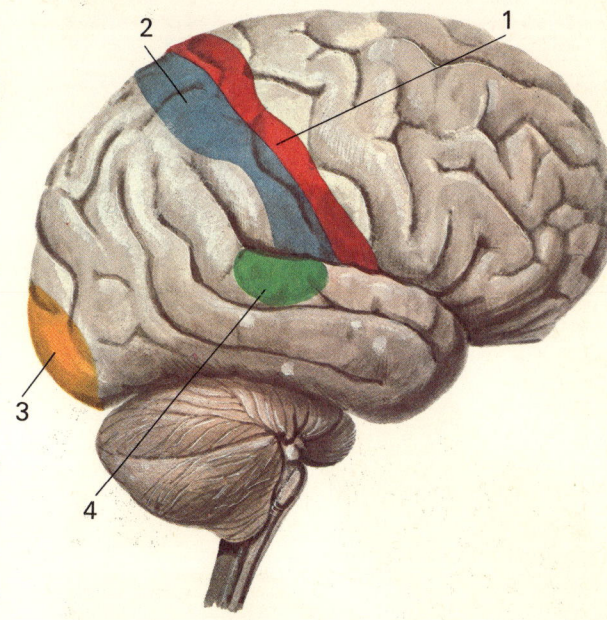

Above: The human brain. The brain is located at the upper end of the spinal column, and weighs just over 1 kilo. It consists of a number of parts.

The cerebrum is large, and extends backward, partially covering the rest of the brain. Its surface has many folds, and therefore its area is larger than it looks. It consists of two halves, known as the *cerebral hemispheres*.

The cerebrum is responsible for sensation, intelligence, and emotion. The numbers indicate its various parts:
1. The motor area.
2. The sensory area, for heat, cold, touch, pressure.
3. The visual area.
4. The hearing area.

Below the cerebrum is the cerebellum, also made up of two halves. This is the area concerned with co-ordination of muscular movement.

Right: The sizes of the brain of different animals are compared.

The capacity of man's brain is greater than that of other primates, and has gradually become more and more developed.

The brain of the australopithecine had a capacity of about 500 c.c.; that of *Homo erectus* from 750–1,200 c.c.; and modern man's brain ranges from 1,000–2,000 c.c.

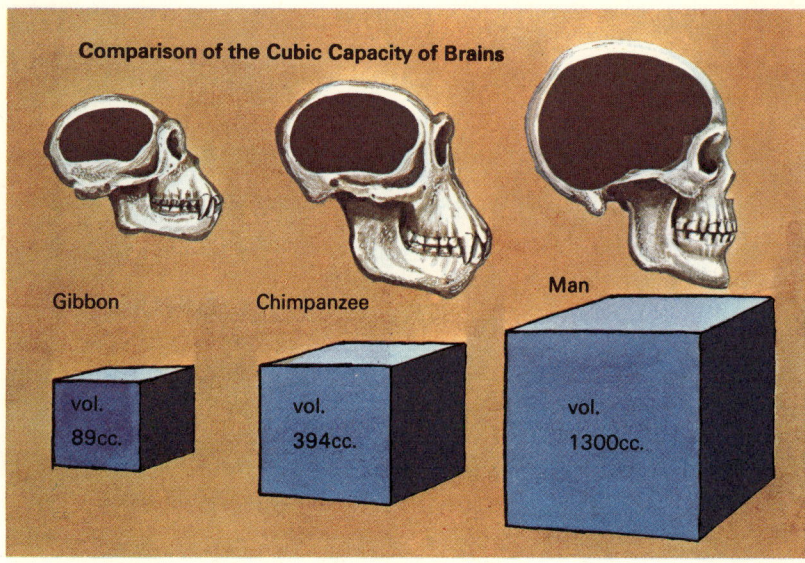

MAN AND THE ANIMAL KINGDOM

In order to study life, it is essential that all living and extinct forms be grouped according to well-defined characteristics or principles.

Classifying the animal and plant kingdoms entails many difficulties.

Animals and plants are grouped into units of increasing specialization. The basic units of the classification scheme are: kingdom, phylum, class, order, family, genus, and species.

Scientists refer to plants and animals by two Latin names, which correspond to the genus and species, and which are always printed in italics. For example, the scientific name of the dog is *Canis familiaris*.

How is modern man classified? No one would doubt that he is a member of the animal kingdom. Within this kingdom are two great groups of animals: those without backbones (the invertebrates), and those with backbones (the vertebrates). Man, having a backbone, belongs to the phylum of which this is a characteristic.

All mammals are grouped together because they have a number of things in common. They have two sets of teeth during their lifetime; they possess hair; they suckle their young; they are warm-blooded. Man can therefore be placed in the class Mammalia.

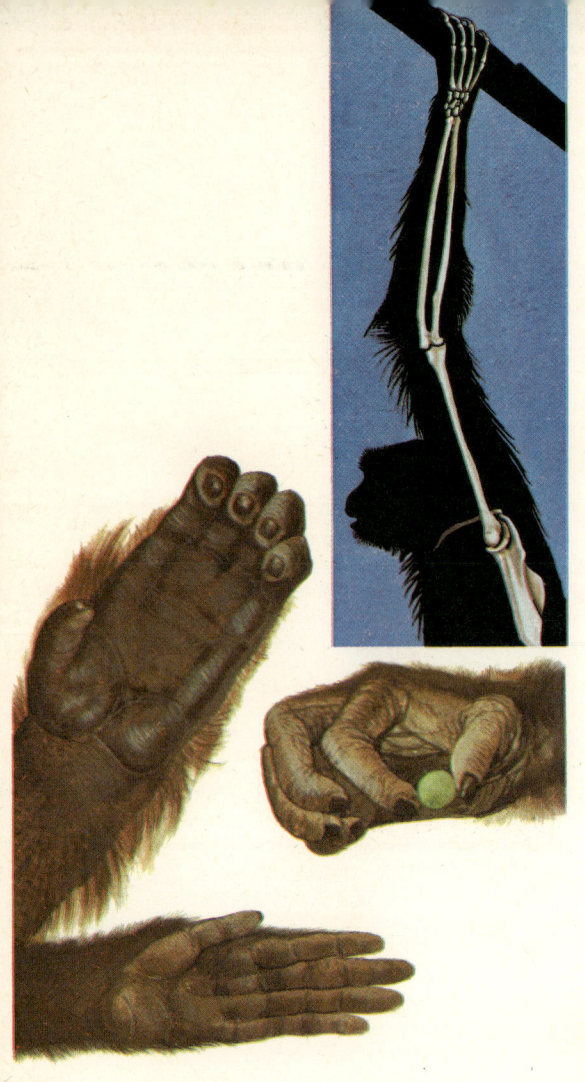

Above: The primates are able to grasp objects.
The original claws have been replaced by nails, which help to support the finger pads.

Right: The evolution of some of the mammalian groups.
The first mammals appeared in the Triassic Period, some 200 million years ago. They remained small and inconspicuous for millions of years.
By the middle of Cretaceous times, ancestors of present-day marsupials in Australia were already there.
At the end of the Cretaceous Period, the stage was set for the rapid development of the mammals.
By Eocene times, all the main groups were represented. (Examples are the four groups shown in the diagram.) Some of the groups would spawn new groups, some of which were destined to die out; others still live on today. The primates, from their lowly beginnings, have gone on to rule the world, in the form of man. Perhaps if the primate group had not been so successful, the rodents or some other group would now be the dominant form of life on earth.

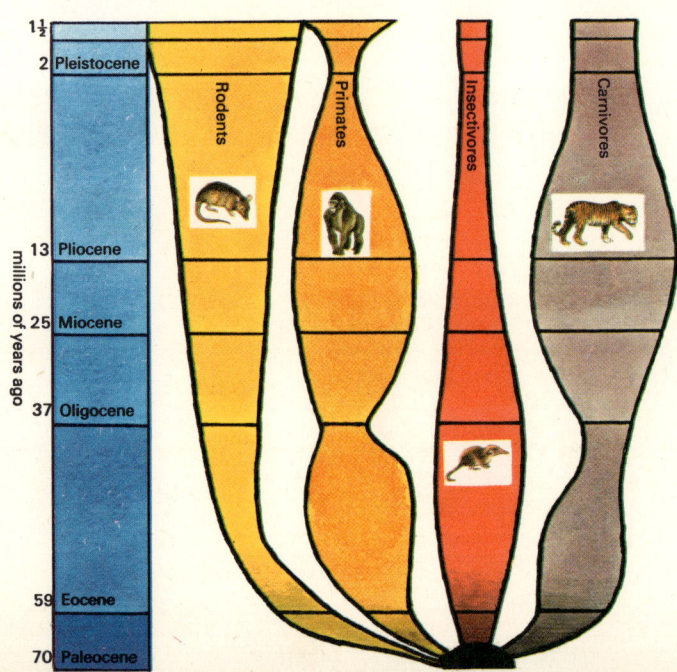

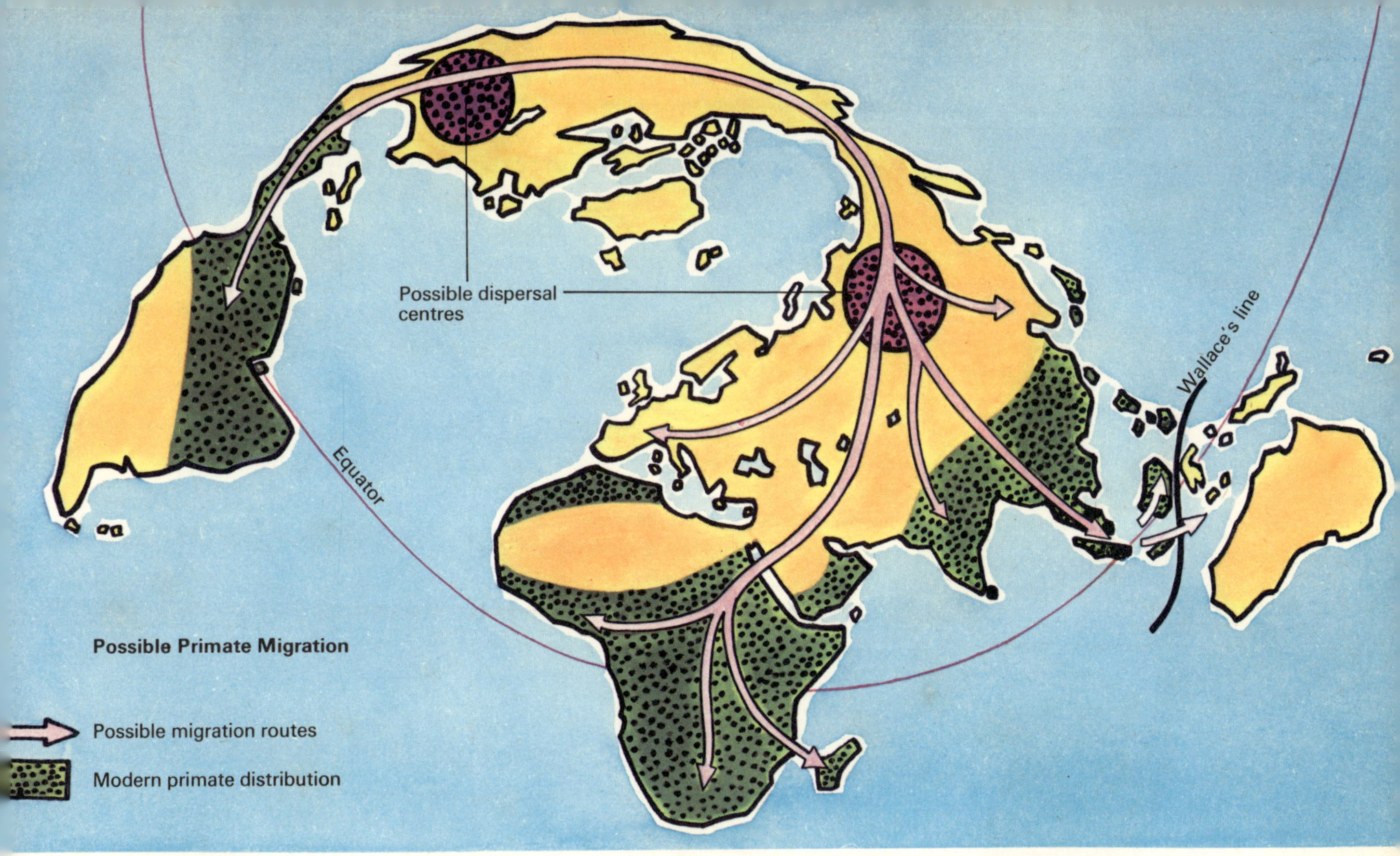

Another group of characteristics leads to the order known as primates. Animals so classed live in trees or have near-relatives that did; they must have the ability to grasp, and must possess forward-looking eyes. The animals of this group mostly see in depth.

In most members of the primates, claws have been replaced by flat nails which help to support the finger pads.

The entire group shows a progressive increase in brain capacity.

Not all animals classified as primates have these characteristics, but certainly man does.

Above: The migration of the primates. Even the earliest primates were widely distributed throughout the world. Their development reached a peak in Eocene times, and has declined since then.

The early primates, which have evolved in South America into New World monkeys, must have reached that continent by means of "island-hopping", since at that time North and South America were not joined by land.

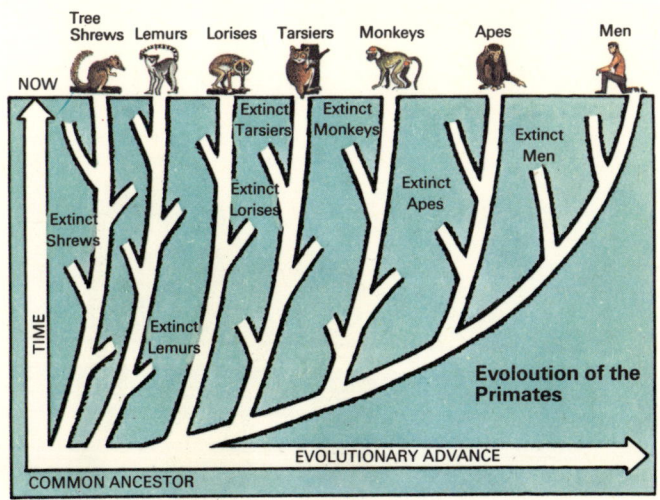

Left: The evolution of the primates from a common ancestor.

The first primates must have appeared at the very end of Cretaceous times, and probably resembled the tree shrews of today's tropical rain forests. These little creatures resemble their close relatives the insectivores (insect-eating mammals).

It is therefore possible to discern the approximate direction from which the primate origins came. A primate showing more advanced features is the lemur, a creature with eyes directed forward. It does not have claws, so it climbs by gripping.

The order of mammals called the primates includes lemurs, bush babies, tarsiers, monkeys, baboons, gibbons, orang-utans, chimpanzees, gorillas, and men.

The primates themselves are divided into two major groups: one having the more primitive members of the order, the other the more advanced.

The creatures believed to have sufficient human characteristics are grouped into the family known as Hominidae. This family includes modern man, the prehistoric man of the Far East, Neanderthal man, and the australopithecines.

A species is a group of animals which resemble each other and are able to breed with one another and to produce offspring, which in turn can also breed with one another. The palaeontologist's difficulty in classifying animals at this level is readily apparent.

Species with a similar ancestry are grouped into a particular genus.

Man can therefore be classified as follows:

KINGDOM:	Animalia
PHYLUM:	Chordata
CLASS:	Mammalia
ORDER:	Primates
FAMILY:	Hominidae
GENUS:	*Homo*
SPECIES:	*sapiens*

The correct scientific name for modern man is therefore *Homo sapiens*. Many authorities believe that modern man is a separate subspecies, and should be designated *Homo sapiens sapiens*.

Another subspecies of man is Neanderthal man, whose correct name is *Homo sapiens neanderthalensis*.

The species is a unit which evolves. Species show variation. Without this variation, evolution could not take place, because there would be nothing for natural selection to act upon.

THE RISE OF THE PRIMATES

The primates developed some 70 million years ago at the close of the Mesozoic Era. This was indeed a time of great change.

The Mesozoic Era had been the era of the reptiles. The great dinosaurs dominated the land and the mammals remained small. At the end of the Cretaceous Period the dinosaurs suddenly died out. The reasons for their extinction are not fully known, although there have been many theories.

Cretaceous times were followed by a period in which lush forests grew up throughout the world. Tropical and temperate conditions were more widespread than today. The flora of southern England resembled that of present-day Malaya.

Into this new world came the mammals. They had already been on the earth for millions of years, but now they were destined to develop and become the dominant form of life.

Above: *Notharctus*, an early type of primate which is somewhat like the lemur. It dates from Eocene times and comes from North America.

Below: Distribution of primates today (other than man) is shown on the map. The Old World monkeys are found throughout Africa, India, and the Far East, but such forms as lemurs and tree shrews have a limited distribution.

Apes are represented in the Far East by the gibbon and the orang-utan, and in Africa by the gorilla and chimpanzee.

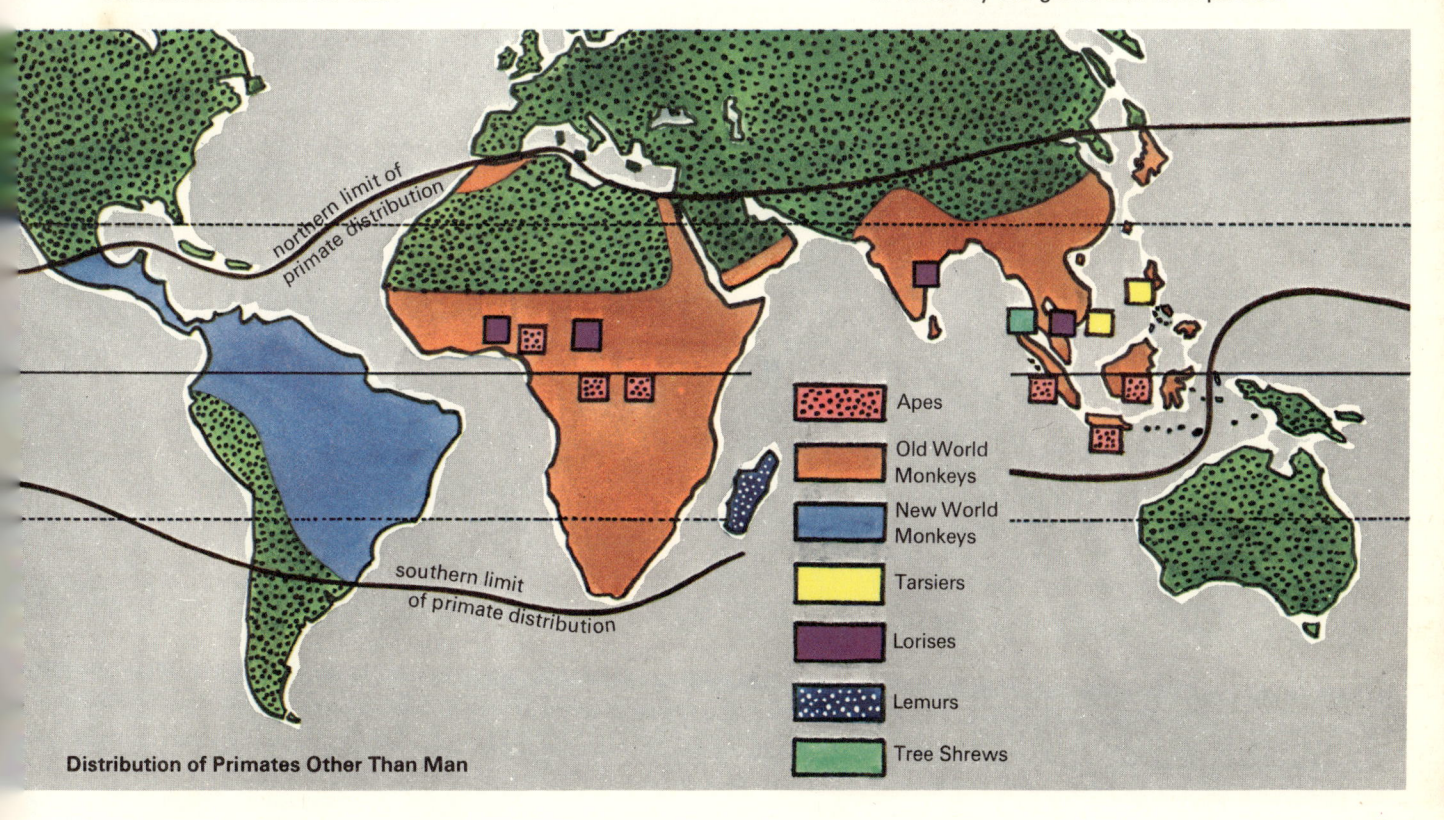

Distribution of Primates Other Than Man

- Apes
- Old World Monkeys
- New World Monkeys
- Tarsiers
- Lorises
- Lemurs
- Tree Shrews

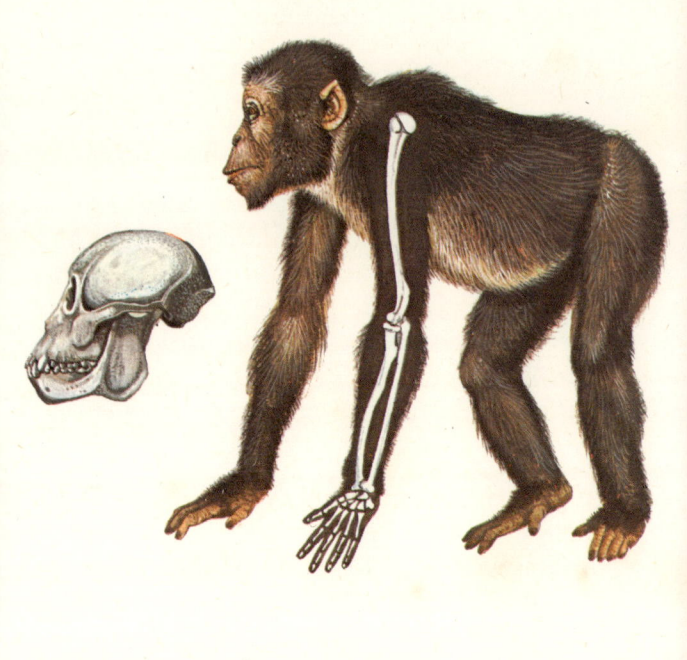

Above: A forest has definite layers, and each one has its own particular form of life. The primates of the various layers show certain adaptations to their ways of life.

There are the ground dwellers and the shrub-layer dwellers; and those that live in the lowest branches, at the higher levels, and in the uppermost branches of the tallest trees.

The primates most likely evolved from the insectivores. An example of a modern insectivore is the hedgehog.

The Palaeocene primates do not seem to have developed greatly and, although some lived on into Eocene times, most of them disappeared earlier.

In Eocene times a more advanced primate appeared on the scene. It has been suggested that this new type of primate arose because of competition from rodents, which also began to develop at this time. Perhaps, therefore, the primates were forced into a new way of life.

Certainly Eocene primates had forward-looking eyes, reduced snouts, and limbs which were adapted to a life in the trees.

The New World and the Old World higher primates developed from more primitive stock in either Eocene or early Oligocene times. In some ways the New World monkeys are more primitive than those of the Old World. It was to be in the Old World however, where evolution was to lead onward to the apes and man.

Left: The so-called *Proconsul africanus*, a Miocene ape. The illustration depicts the upper limb and skull. This ape has been known to exist since 1926. Its skull, discovered in 1948, was the first skull palaeontologists had seen of any Miocene ape. The remains were found on Rusinga Island, Lake Victoria, Kenya, as well as on other shores of the lake. The ape is now classified as a member of the genus *Dryopithecus*. This genus was very widespread; remains have been discovered in Asia and Europe as well as Africa.

Right: A reconstruction of *Oreopithecus*.

In 1958, a most unusual event took place. From the Baccinello Mine, in Grosseto, Italy, came an almost complete skeleton of *Oreopithecus*, a higher primate that had been known for about a hundred years by means of various bone fragments. The deposits in which the new remains were found are brown coal (lignite) from the Pliocene period. The unfortunate ape, making its way through the trees, must have somehow fallen to its death in the swamps. It was an ideal medium for preservation, and therefore a propitious fall for palaeontologists.

Oreopithecus had long arms and was about the size of a chimpanzee.

Various studies of the skeleton indicate that the animal could have walked upright. Originally, scientists thought this ape, dubbed "the abominable coalman", might be a direct ancestor of man, but further research did not support this theory.

THE APES COME

The remains of primates from the Oligocene deposits are found mainly in the Fayum region of Egypt. The deposits here are about 26–28 million years old, and although the area is now a desert, during Oligocene times it was a tropical forest area through which many rivers flowed.

Fossils have been found which may be ancestors of either the Old World monkeys or *Oreopithecus*, the ape fossil recovered from the brown coal deposits of Italy. Until such discoveries were made, the origin of the Old World monkeys was obscure.

One of the most interesting finds at Fayum is called *Aegyptopithecus*. It is believed that this specimen could have been a forerunner of the lines of descent which led to the apes and man.

A specimen which poses some difficulties in classification is called *Propliopithecus*. This could have been an ancestor of *Aegyptopithecus*, or it could have developed into the line which includes *Ramapithecus*. Another possibility is that it gave rise to the *dryopithecines* and, through various other forms, to man.

As far back as Oligocene times there were developments which would lead to the forerunners of the modern apes, and possibly the beginning of the line from which man himself is descended.

Apes appeared, notably in Asia and Africa, during Miocene times, but there is little evidence of monkeys. All fossil apes of this period possibly may be grouped into the one genus *Dryopithecus*.

Remains have also been found in Europe. The size of these animals varied greatly, ranging from that of a gibbon to that of a gorilla.

Lines of descent from certain members of the dryopithecines to the present-day gorilla and chimpanzee have been established. Possibly another line of descent was that which led to *Ramapithecus*.

The Pliocene Epoch holds in store the largest primate of all. Possibly evolving from dryopithecine stock and adapted to a non-forest environment, *Gigantopithecus* appeared in India and China. This immense beast was probably nearly three metres tall and weighed nearly three hundred kilos. He continued well into the Pleistocene.

As we move onward toward more modern times, one creature must lay claim to being on man's line of evolution, or at least close to it. Some experts would contend that it is the earliest hominid. Again, possibly evolving from the dryopithecines, *Ramapithecus* has many interesting features.

The canine teeth are reduced in size, and the dental arcade is similar to those of early men. Much significance has been given to the fragmentary remains of this higher primate. Nevertheless, many more specimens must be examined and analysed before we can be certain that this is an ancestor of the australopithecines.

Finds have also been made in Kenya of a form similar to *Ramapithecus*.

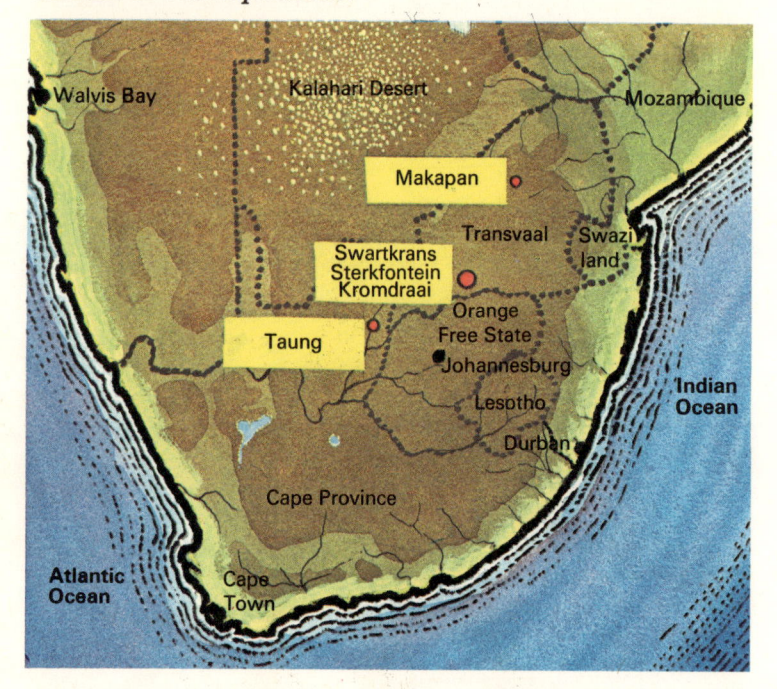

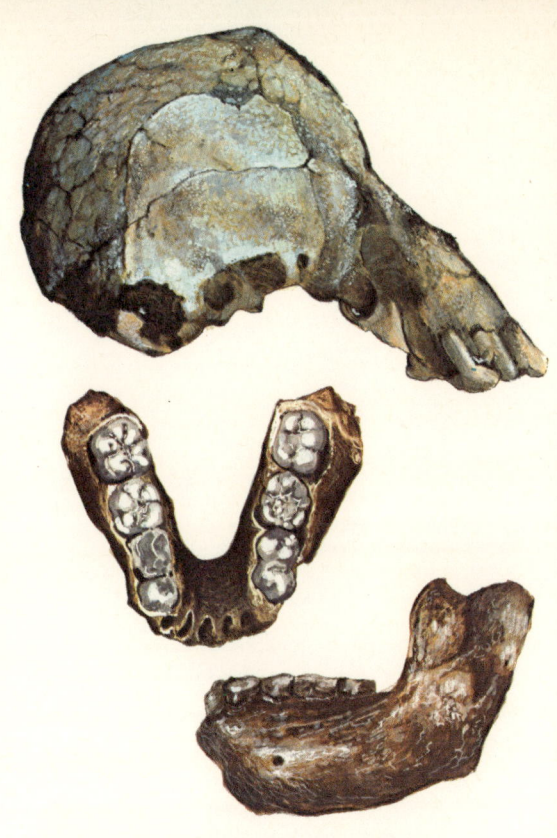

Above: Australopithecine finds at Makapansgat include skulls, lower jaws, and other remains. The first specimens were discovered in 1948 and investigated by Professor Raymond Dart.

The Makapansgat site is more recent than the other sites in South Africa, which have yielded remains of a gracile (slender) australopithecine. It was at this site that scientists originally thought they had found evidence of the use of fire.

Left: Various sites in South Africa have yielded remains of two types of early hominid. The remains at Taung, Sterkfontein, and Makapansgat, are of the gracile form, while those from Swartkrans and Kromdraai are of the robust form.

It has always been difficult to date these deposits, but it would seem that the oldest are those at Sterkfontein and Taung, while Makapansgat, Swartkrans, and Kromdraai are successively younger.

THE ANCESTORS OF MAN

Man's gradual development away from the evolutionary line which led onward to the apes has been shown to have come about many millions of years ago.

Man himself has gradually accumulated a wealth of knowledge about the world in which he lives. He has also learned much of the earth's past history. Many fossils have been found, although not enough of prehistoric man have been recovered so that their evolution may be fully understood. There are many mysterious gaps in the saga of man's advancement. A very long gap exists between the primate *Ramapithecus* described earlier, and the first creatures which are accepted as hominids.

Of course, it may well be that *Ramapithecus* will attain the status of a hominid itself in the future. Possibly this will also apply to related African specimens.

Before that can happen, though, if it ever does, many more specimens must be made available for scientific study. Much work in the field, under hard conditions, and many hours of painstaking work in the laboratory will be required.

Since the term hominid will occur frequently in this text, it is necessary to describe what is meant by it.

The family group to which modern man belongs is called Hominidae. Thus, any members of this family are known as hominids. They may not be in the same genus as modern man, but they will have numerous similarities.

For as long as man has been able to think and reason he has had a consuming interest in the origin of his species.

Many of man's myths and religions have stemmed from this desire to know more of his past. It took a long time for even a little of this fascinating tale to be revealed. Even now, much is still not clear, but at least the basic lines of evolution are established.

It was preconceived ideas about man's development in past ages which allowed the infamous Piltdown forgery to become so widely accepted.

In a gravel pit of a small village named Piltdown

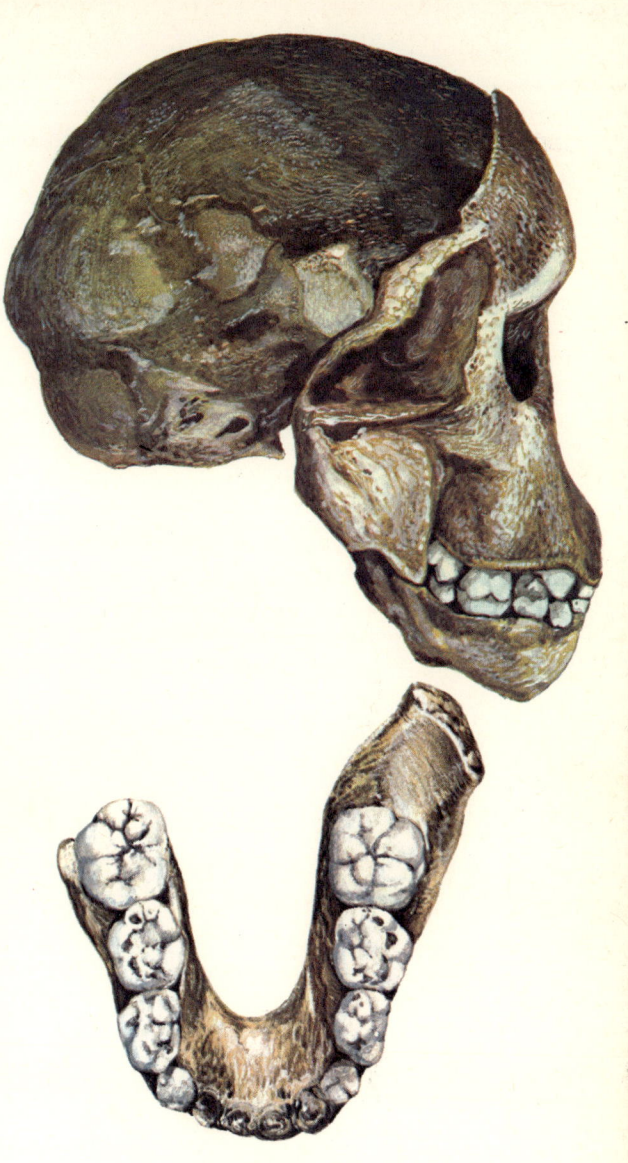

Above: This skull and its mandible belonged to a gracile australopithecine. They were discovered at Taung, in South Africa, and are a little over 2 million years old.

(in east Sussex in England) a skull resembling that of modern man was found connected to an ape-like jaw. These finds were made in 1912, and additional fragments came to light some years later.

Thus was produced what many had hoped for in prehistoric man: a brain the same size as modern man's with ape-like features.

Many years later, in 1953, it was finally proved by fluorine tests that the skull of Piltdown man was indeed that of a modern man, but the jaw was that of an ape with suitable modifications. In short, it was a "fake".

This sort of fraud could not now remain undetected because of modern dating methods. But in the 1920s, it was Piltdown man which to some extent prevented general acceptance of the first finds of true hominids in South Africa.

OBSTACLES IN FINDING FOSSIL MAN

There are many difficulties to be overcome in trying to trace the relations of man. Fragments of prehistoric man are rarely found in any particular order. It is unlikely that complete skeletons will be discovered. It is more likely that the few remains which can be found at a site will be broken or deformed. And because man lives on land, the chances of his remains being preserved or fossilized are immediately reduced.

Early man undoubtedly had many physical and cultural variations as do men today; but it is now most difficult to know whether specimens from different localities really belong to the same species. They may even be subspecies.

Below: Fragments of a gracile australopithecine from Makapansgat, South Africa. Included are pelvic and skull bones. It is from this location that remains of both male and female pelvic girdles have been recovered.

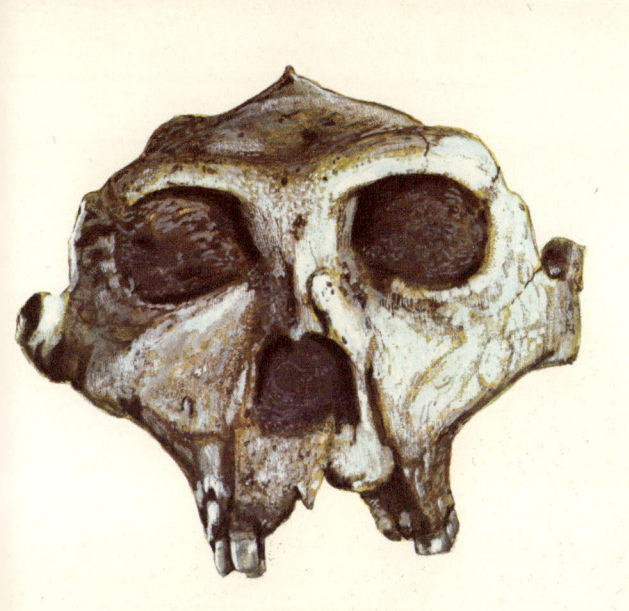

Above: The cave deposits at Swartkrans are noted for the remains of the robust form of australopithecine recovered from them.
 The best skull and a hipbone are illustrated. The skull has a crest on top for the attachment of the large muscles which were needed to operate the heavy jaws.
 Many teeth have also been recovered from this site.

Far left: The best-preserved skull of the gracile form of australopithecine, found at Sterkfontein. Tools have also been recovered from this site.

Left: One of the most important finds at Sterkfontein was this incomplete pelvis. The pelvis has certain resemblances to that of modern man, as well as that of the great apes.

In some areas of the world (for example, Europe) which have been well surveyed geologically, finds of fossils have been large. In regions of lesser development, survey work may be just beginning, but will yield relics of tremendous importance in man's evolution.

In areas which already have been adequately mapped geologically and topographically, it is easier to understand the relationship of fragments of fossil man which might be found, since their geological horizon and age will be accurately known.

Even so, in some areas (such as in South Africa, where there are many important sites) it is still quite difficult to date the remains. Even if dating is possible, there is still a need to correlate information on deposits of supposedly similar age in different parts of the world in order to understand fully the evolution of man.

Matters have not been made any easier by the scientists themselves. For many years there was a tendency to label almost every new find as either a new genus or species of fossil man. New names and designations were abundant, and only recently has the situation become a little clearer.

In some ways our knowledge of early man has had to wait until first-hand information could be obtained on other primates. Studies on present-day primates have become more and more intensive over the last few years. By observing and almost living with such animals as chimpanzees and gorillas out in the field, scientists have gained much valuable knowledge.

THE EARLIEST MEN

For our first glimpse of the earliest hominids we must go back thousands of years to Africa. Evolution has progressed far. A creature moving across the open plain walks in an upright way, but perhaps not as well as we can – he certainly does not drop down onto all fours.

Perhaps if we survey a large enough area, which includes both plain and lightly-wooded country, we shall observe another early ancestor of man.

To start with, there are two types of hominid, not just one. Both types are given the generic name *Australopithecus* by some authorities. There are other authorities, however, who view them as separate genera.

These two forms have caused a great deal of discussion in scientific circles, but gradually the picture of their way of life and their differences has emerged.

Above: Representatives of the first undisputed group of the family of man, the australopithecines. Though less agile than modern man, they certainly did not walk on all fours, as did some animals in the primate group. Their normal way of moving and living was in an upright position.

The smaller form is slender and lithe and often known as a gracile australopithecine. Scientifically, he is called *Australopithecus africanus*, the southern ape of Africa. This gracile form has been discovered in deposits which may be as old as five million years.

The more robust form was a much heavier creature with larger face and jaws. Even so, he walked upright. The scientific name for the robust form is *Paranthropus*. The gracile form was about 1·4 metres tall, and weighed about thirty kilos, while the larger form was over 1·5 metres and tipped the scales at over forty-five kilos.

So far as the gracile creature is concerned, he was a plains dweller. He made his camp by the river so that he had a ready supply of water. A rock shelter or cave might have been used as a temporary home. It is known that he had meat in his diet, so he must have hunted game in some way.

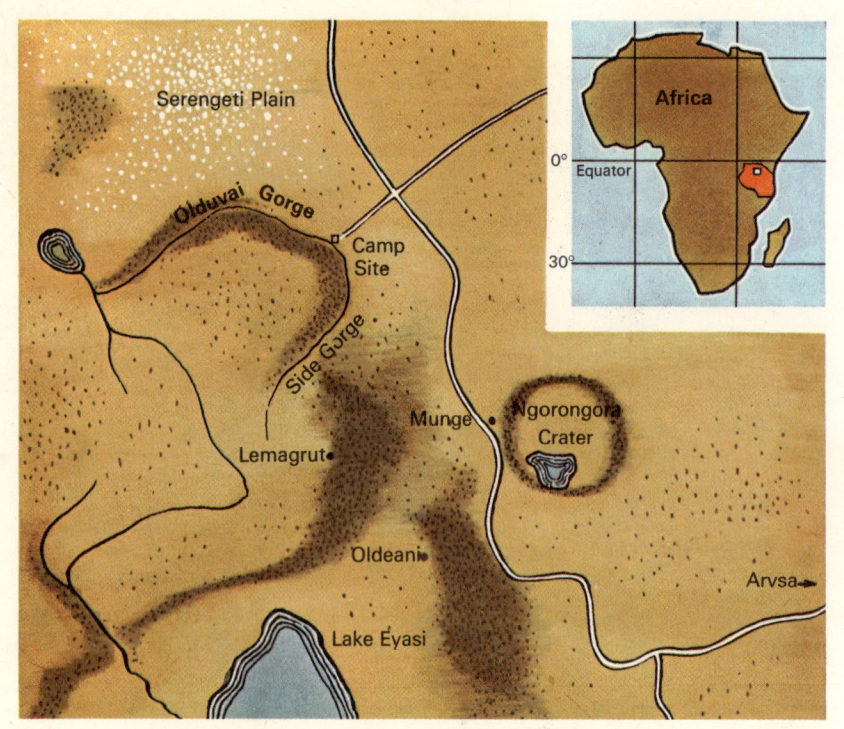

Left: The world's most important site for discovering fossil man is undoubtedly Olduvai Gorge, situated on the Serengeti Plain, Tanzania.

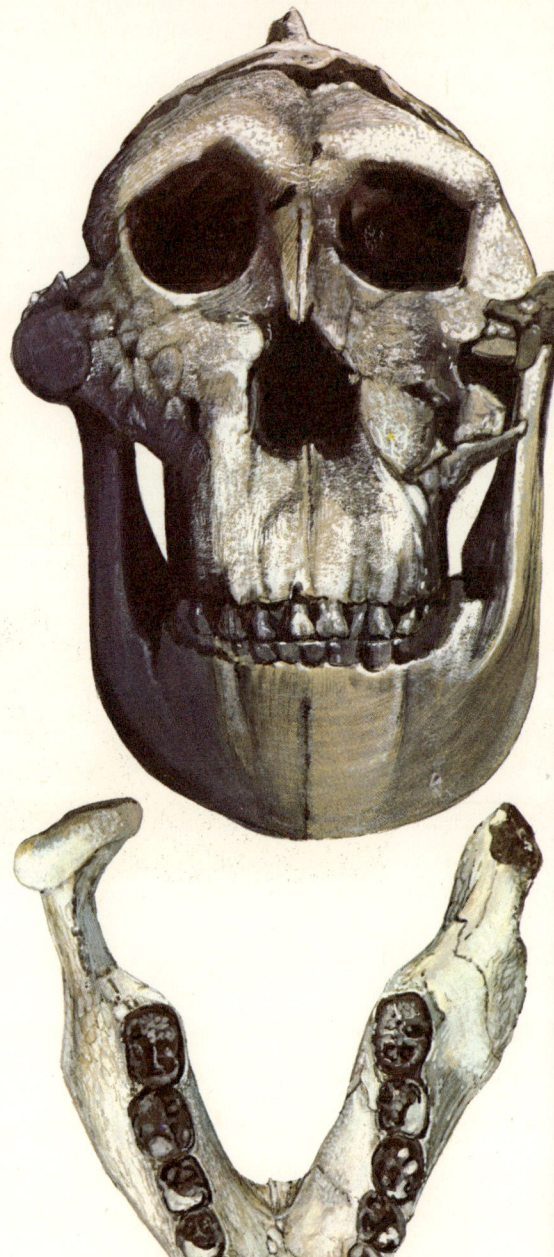

Tools are believed to have been made by this early hominid, and at least one palaeontologist thinks that bone, tooth and horn were materials used.

It is thought that they generally lived in small groups, continually on the move: the women and children looking for roots and suitable fruits, while the men gave protection to them and hunted for meat. If this was the case, then there must have been co-operation between members of a group.

One scientist has calculated that an average age at death was 18, although some individuals lived to the age of 40. It would seem that these primitive societies first had children in their early teens.

THE SOUTH AFRICAN FINDS

Remains of both the robust and gracile forms have been discovered in the Republic of South Africa. The gracile forms were found at Taung, Sterkfontein and Makapansgat. The sites at Swartkrans and Kromdraai have provided fragments of the more robust creatures. These sites have proved difficult to date, but it is generally accepted that the sites at Taung and Sterkfontein are about two million years old, while those at Makapansgat, Swartkrans, and Kromdraai are successively younger, Kromdraai being just a little under a million years old.

Above: Originally named *Zinjanthropus*, this specimen was found by Dr. Mary Leakey. It is shown here with a reconstructed lower jaw, which is based on the one discovered at Peninj.

This so-called Natron jaw, from Lake Natron, which is near Peninj, is pictured below the skull. The specimen is now considered to be an australopithecine, because of its large face and heavy features.

THE EAST AFRICAN FINDS

East Africa, where the famous Olduvai Gorge and Omo sites are found, has provided a great deal of material. From the remains at Lothagam Hill it has been concluded that the more delicate form of australopithecine is at least five million years old, while specimens only a little younger have also been found at Kanapoi, north-western Kenya.

Omo, a site in Ethiopia, has tremendous potential for the remains of fossil man. An international team has been hard at work here since 1967. Remains of the less robust australopithecines have already been discovered, as well as other hominids.

The names of the world-famous Dr L. S. B. Leakey and his wife are synonymous with Olduvai Gorge. With their co-workers they have discovered

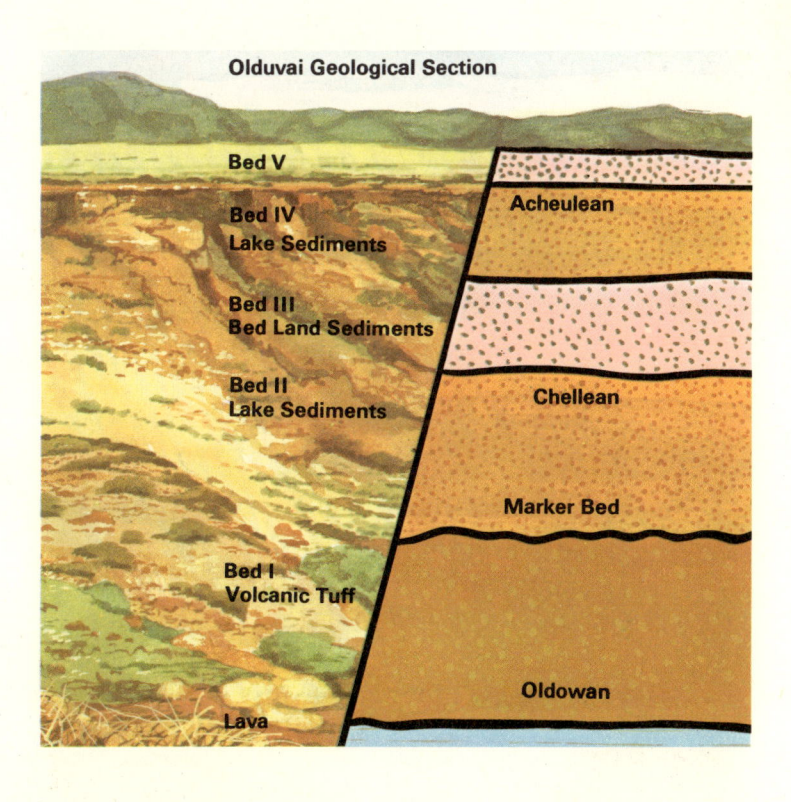

Left: Perhaps the best-known geological section is that of Olduvai Gorge. Five beds have been recognized, numbered upwards from the oldest, Bed I.

The section is made up of lake and volcanic deposits. Lake deposits are ideal for the preservation of fossils, and the rocks from the volcanic outbursts yield good material for accurate dating.

much valuable material and added greatly to our knowledge of man's ancestors.

The river has cut a gorge, some three hundred feet deep, through lake and volcanic deposits, to make Olduvai Gorge. These deposits are excellent for the preservation of fossils, and the volcanic rocks provide material which allows an accurate guide to dates.

Below and right: Below the bed where *Zinjanthropus* was discovered, and therefore geologically older than *Zinjanthropus*, a skull and other fragments were discovered, in 1960, by Dr. Leakey's team. These, together with other remains from the higher, and therefore younger Bed II, were believed to be not australopithecines, but a species of man. He was named *Homo habilis*. The illustration shows the skull from Bed II, (below), and, (right), a comparison between it and a skull of modern man.

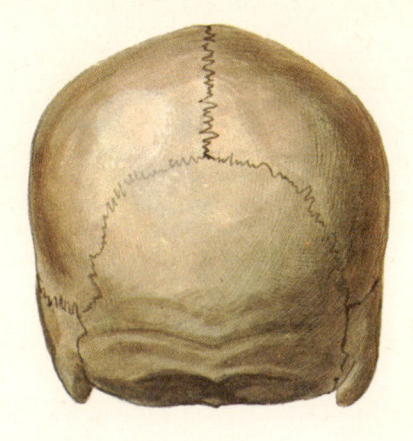

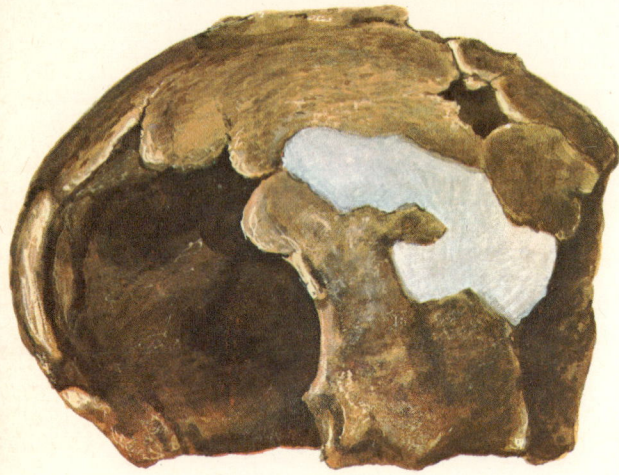

Right: A reconstruction of *Homo habilis*, considered by some to be an australopithecine.

Left: The quarry of Dragon Hill, Choukoutien, a site where fossil teeth were first discovered in 1921. In 1927, Davidson Black audaciously reconstructed *Sinanthropus pekinensis* from a single tooth.

Regarded by most as a subspecies of *Homo erectus*, the object of Dr. Black's interest is popularly known as *Peking Man*.

After Black's discovery, skull remains and many other fragments were found.

The site has also yielded remains of deer, rhinoceros, and other mammals.

Tools, too, have been discovered here, as well as the first evidence of man using fire.

The deposits are of the Middle Pleistocene age.

The site is located about 25 miles south-west of Peking.

The Silurian limestone is riddled with caves and cavities, which were opened by quarrying operations. As shown in the illustration, the site was divided into fifteen sections, in order to obtain accurate records of the finds to be plotted.

The sequence of rocks in the Gorge has been divided into five beds, Bed I being the oldest. Remains of a large australopithecine have been found in Bed I and are dated as about 1,750,000 years old.

From a slightly lower level, and therefore older deposit, have come the remains of a hominid which has caused some controversy in the scientific world. The new find was given the name *Homo habilis*, which means able or skilful man, and is regarded by some experts as being more advanced than the australopithecines. Indeed, because of various features, it is seen as a member of the same genus as present-day man. Other remains of this creature have also been found at Olduvai.

Remains of the larger australopithecine, not unlike those from Swartkrans, have been found by Richard Leakey at Peninj. Other remains have come from near Lake Rudolf.

Before the true relationships of all material found in East and South Africa are known, a more painstaking search will have to be undertaken. Until the pieces of the puzzle fit together completely we know only that hominids have lived in Africa for some five million years, and that several different populations may be represented.

Whether or not *Homo habilis* will prove to be a local variation of the South African gracile australopithecines, or whether it represents a step forward to modern man, will only be known as more fragments of prehistoric man are unearthed and studied.

MEN OF THE MIDDLE PLEISTOCENE

The men of these times lived from some 350,000 to one million years ago. The first specimens were discovered in the Far East near the end of the nineteenth century by Eugene Dubois. Dubois went out especially to look for fossils of man, and indeed discovered them in Java in the gravel of the banks of the Solo River.

The men of these times have been called pithecanthropines – and individual finds have given rise to Peking Man and Java Man. They are all now believed to be of the same genus and species, *Homo erectus*, although subspecies are recognized. This means, of course that they are considered to be far enough advanced to be placed in the same genus as modern man.

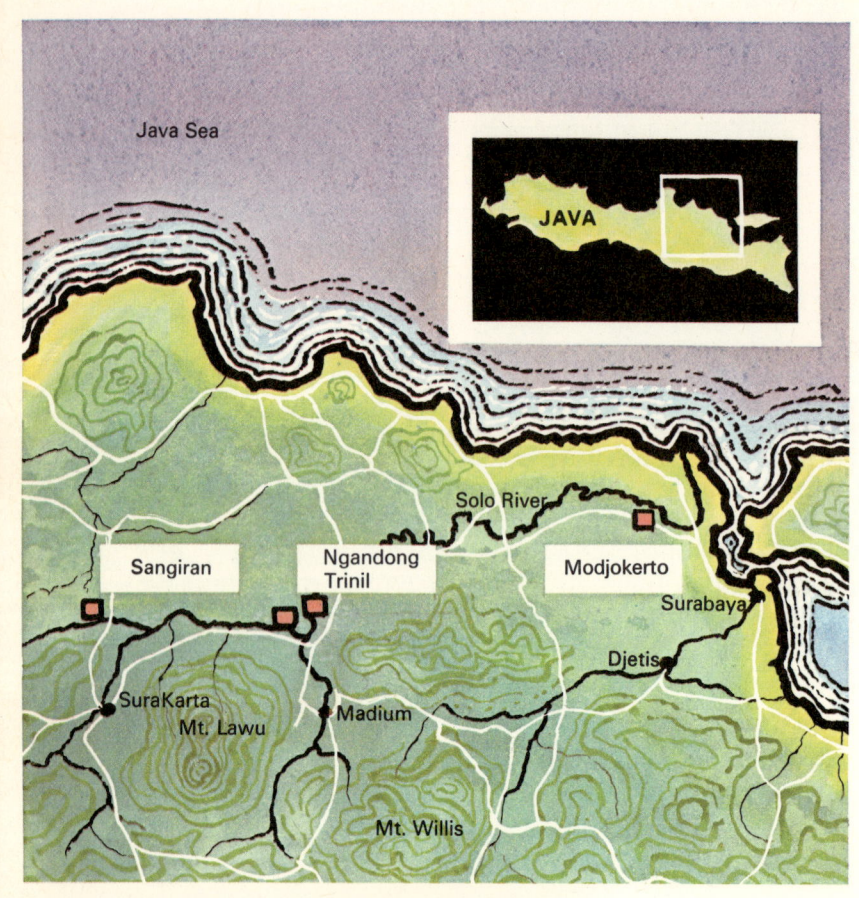

Left: Map illustrating the various sites in Java at which the remains of early man have been discovered. One of the first fossils was found in Trinil. Those from Sangiran, though older, resemble those of Trinil.

The skull of a small child was found at Modjokerto. All of the illustrations represent finds of pithecanthropines. In Ngandong, the remains of a more advanced form of man have been found.

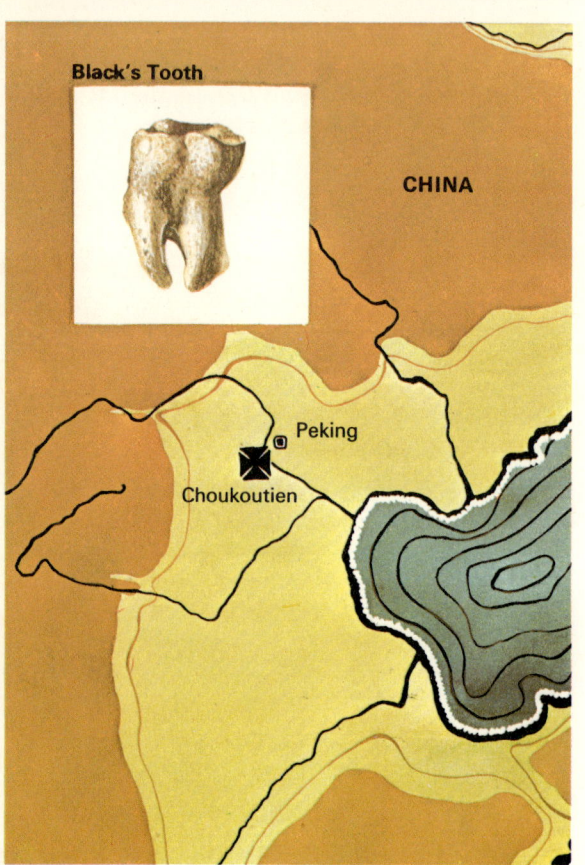

Left: Dr. Davidson Black's site near Peking, together with the tooth that was the basis for his description of a new type of prehistoric man.

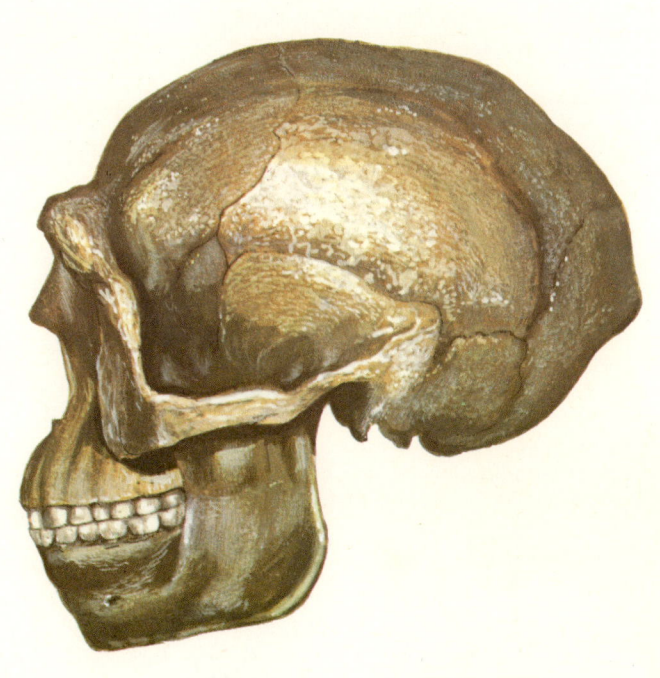

Above: A cast of a Peking adult female.

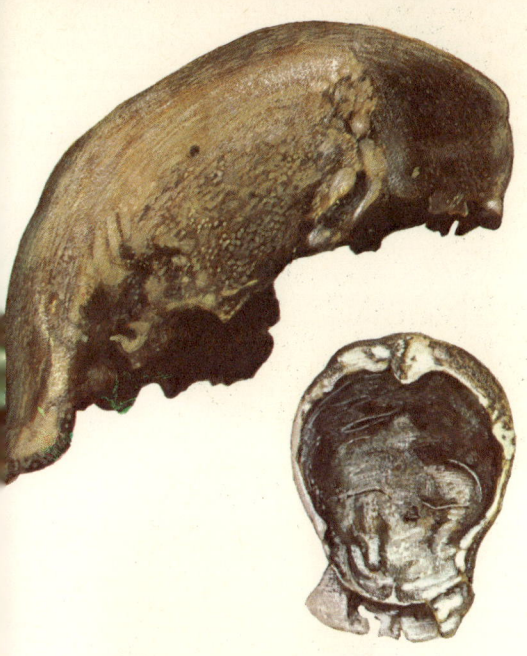

Above: Side and internal views of a skull from Trinil.

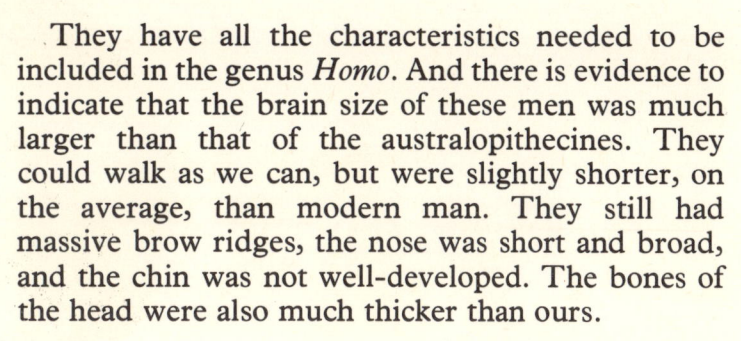

They have all the characteristics needed to be included in the genus *Homo*. And there is evidence to indicate that the brain size of these men was much larger than that of the australopithecines. They could walk as we can, but were slightly shorter, on the average, than modern man. They still had massive brow ridges, the nose was short and broad, and the chin was not well-developed. The bones of the head were also much thicker than ours.

They made tools of a more advanced type and possessed one great advantage over their predecessors: they knew how to use fire. How fire came to be used by man is not really known, nor is it known when he became able to start it at will.

Fire can be terrifying, and many prehistoric men must have witnessed its effects by watching volcanoes or lightning flashes. Perhaps he even created it by accident when sparks from two flints fell onto dry grass.

Once he learned to control fire, the usefulness was extended. Fire could warm the cave and provide light. This latter feature could be of value to man in manufacturing his tools. Fire would also keep away wild animals.

Certainly if men could not start it themselves, the fire would be tended with great care once it had been established to keep it going at all times. And if they moved their home the fire might have been taken with them.

The fire would enable them to cook the meat. How cooking began is not known either. It can be imagined, however, that prehistoric man may have come upon the roasted meat of animals after a bush fire. Perhaps he tasted it and liked it better than raw meat. Or perhaps the answer is that, once he had fire in the cave, meat might accidentally have been dropped or left near the fire and become cooked as a result.

Because prehistoric men were such successful hunters, it is possible that they had some form of

Left: The earliest example of disease in man is shown by this leg bone. Perhaps as a result of injury, the upper part of the bone grew into what was the surrounding tissue.

49

Right: Illustration of the remains of the infant found at Modjokerto, by Professor von Koenigswald in 1936. It is generally estimated that the child died at the age of two, although some authorities think he was older. The characteristics of the group to which he belongs, the pithecanthropines, are highly developed, and the remains are from older deposits than those of Trinil.

Below: Peking Man tends his fire. This important new discovery for man must have been treated with great care.

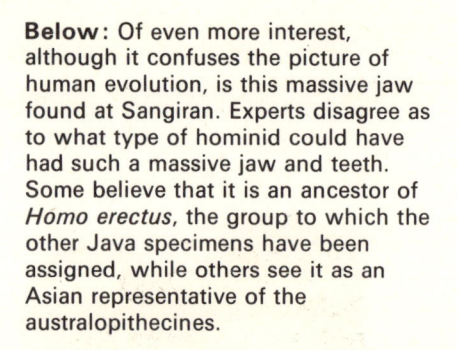

Below: Of even more interest, although it confuses the picture of human evolution, is this massive jaw found at Sangiran. Experts disagree as to what type of hominid could have had such a massive jaw and teeth. Some believe that it is an ancestor of *Homo erectus*, the group to which the other Java specimens have been assigned, while others see it as an Asian representative of the australopithecines.

language. There would be a real need for good communication between members of a hunting party. If groups co-operated on a hunt, then such communications would be even more vital to the well-being of all members.

There certainly was a division of labour between the sexes. The males would provide protection and

Above: A reconstruction of *Heidelberg Man* in typical surroundings. Here he is trying to supplement his diet of roots and fruits with some meat.

The climate during that first interglacial period was mild.

Many animals that no longer live there roamed Europe at the time.

hunt animals, while the women would look after the young and prepare food. They also gathered fruits and roots.

Subsequent to the finds by Dubois, Professor von Koenigswald discovered fragments of *Homo erectus* in somewhat younger deposits. There is also evidence to suggest that another type of hominid was also present in Java at this time, perhaps an australopithecine.

Other Middle Pleistocene men have been found in the limestone caves near Peking in China, which have definite similarities to those found in Java. In Bed II at Olduvai there are similar remains. The Swartkrans site has also yielded material which is believed by some to be pithecanthropine in type.

Other remains have been found in Algeria and Morocco.

One of the earliest human fossils from Europe may be a representative of *Homo erectus*. The Heidelberg jaw combines both ancient and modern features, and could be intermediate between the pithecanthropines and the later forms of man.

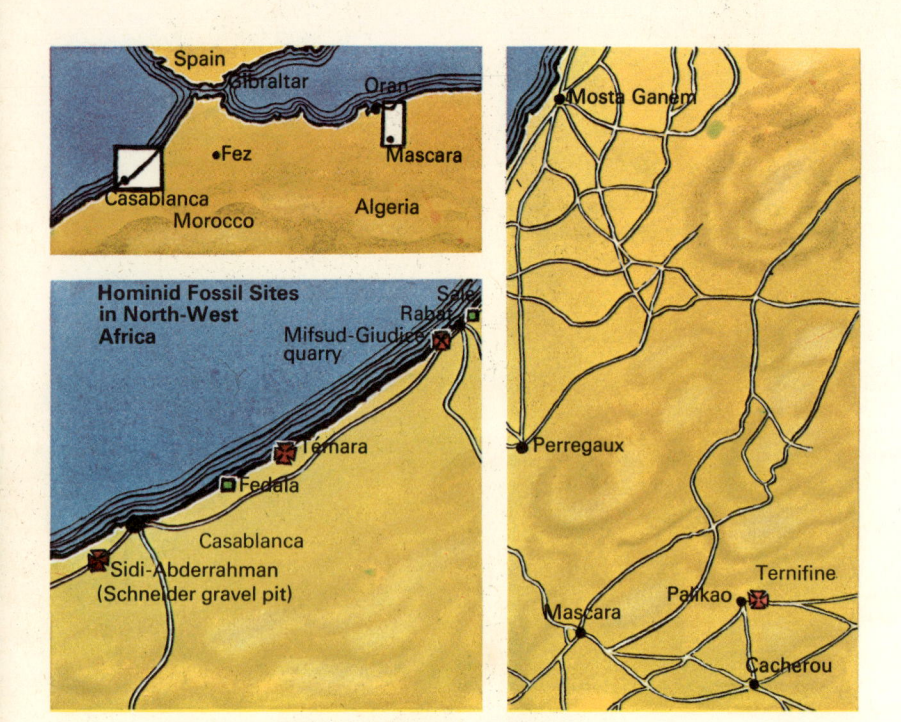

Above: The maps illustrate the various localities in North Africa at which remains of pithecanthropines have been found. The principal site is that at Ternifine, near Mascara, Algeria. Human fossils have also been found in Morocco, at Casablanca and Rabat. The remains at Ternifine were discovered in 1954 and 1955 in rock which had been formed from lake deposits. This bed was discovered while excavating sand from a commercial sandpit.

In the days of prehistoric man the area would have been tropical savanna, replete with elephants, hippopotamus, camels and other animals.

The remains from Casablanca were found in a gravel pit in 1954, while those from Rabat were found in 1933.

THE COMING OF MODERN MAN

The earliest ancestors of *Homo sapiens* (or at least those considered to be) come from various sites, and at present pose a number of problems which will be solved only when further specimens are found.

In Hungary, at Vertesszöllös, are the remains of what is considered to be modern man.

From Swanscombe in England and Steinheim in Germany come the forerunners of *Homo sapiens*. These two finds may be related to each other, and if this is eventually proven to be the case, there was obviously a very widespread early form of modern man.

The direction of evolution from *Homo erectus* is somewhat lost at present, although there are indications in the Far East and elsewhere that the problem may some day be solved.

THE PROBLEM OF NEANDERTHAL MAN

Oddly enough, the problem of Neanderthal man stems from having too many specimens from one area. Fossil collecting really began in Europe in the nineteenth century. From these early days people collected from quarries, river banks and similar places until so much material was available that specialists felt no need to look away from their own area.

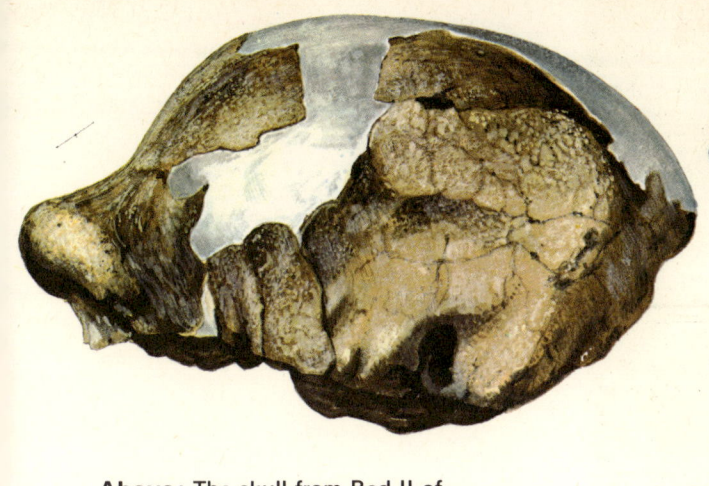

Above: The skull from Bed II of Olduvai Gorge, believed to belong to a pithecanthropine, but precise assessment is still uncertain.

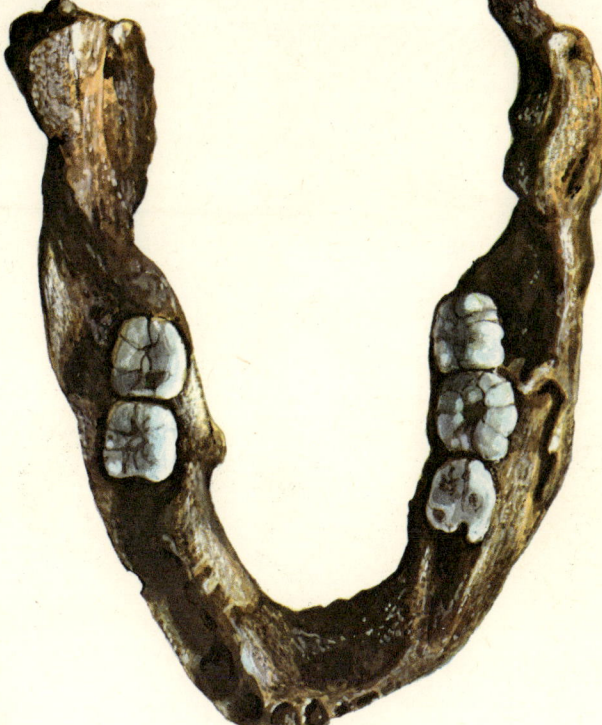

Above: The mandible from Swartkrans, South Africa.

Above: Three views – vertical, internal, and occipital – of the Swanscombe skull. This find, similar to the one at Steinheim in West Germany, seems to indicate a type of man intermediate between *Homo erectus* and modern man.

The brain capacity of Swanscombe man was about 1,325 c.c. The finds were made in 1935, 1936 and 1955 in the hundred-foot terrace of the River Thames. This skull is about 250,000 years old.

It was in Europe, then, that the first discovery of Neanderthal man was made. Quarrying operations unearthed the remains of this now universally known man in the Neander Valley near Düsseldorf in 1856. As the workers had, in fact, thrown the bones away, it was only by good fortune that they were quickly rescued and examined by someone who understood their significance.

Because of the European finds, a rather biased view of this stage in man's evolution was formed. Gradually, however, other parts of the globe were investigated and other remains have come to light to adjust the balance.

It has been shown that the characteristics of Neanderthal man are widespread, and now two forms are recognized: the "classic" neanderthaler, based on the original finds in western Europe, and the progressive type. The latter obviously has many features in common with the "classic" form, but, in the main, their features are not so extreme. They also have characteristics pointing onward to modern

Left: This riverside scene might well have been familiar to Swanscombe man.

It reconstructs his surroundings during the Mindel-Riss interglacial, a long period of time.

Many of the animals that survived from Pliocene times had disappeared and some were to become extinct later.

The climate was obviously milder than it is now in the British Isles, for the remains of Swanscombe man come from Kent, and the banks of the Thames are no longer inhabited by such animals as the elephant and rhinoceros.

man. Even so, the neaderthalers and neanderthaloids are considered a subspecies of our own kind.

The Middle East has produced some very interesting specimens. Two caves at Mount Carmel, Israel, have become particularly famous. Tabūn, the older cave, has yielded remains of man resembling the classic neanderthalers of western Europe, but also bearing features which link him to the discoveries in Africa. A similar find has been made at Shanidar in Iraq.

The other cave at Mount Carmel is called Skūhl. The specimens from here, although resembling the classic Neanderthaler in some ways, definitely have more advanced features reminiscent of modern man.

Neanderthaloid types have also been discovered in South Africa and Asia. The story will eventually be complete when more specimens are found. It will mean that another small gap has been closed in the ancestry of man.

THE ORIGINAL CAVE MAN

The first descriptions of Neanderthal man led to his wide acceptance as the original cave man. We picture him outside his cave, somewhat dim-witted, stooped forward, walking with a shuffle.

He is perhaps the best-known of all the prehistoric men and is popular with cartoonists.

The stereotyped likeness could not be further from the truth. Neanderthal man could walk upright as well as we can. To be sure, he had a rugged look

Above: Part of a skull found at Vertesszöllös, near Budapest, Hungary.

Right: Map showing the location of the Vertesszöllös site.

The human remains from Vertesszöllös were found in 1965, along with mammal remains, small tools, and evidence of the use of fire.

The mammal remains indicate that the time was a warmer phase during the second glacial period.

The remains were found in a tufa layer, which is covered by loess. Tufa is a calcareous deposit left by a spring, while loess is a fine, windblown dust formed when a glacier advances.

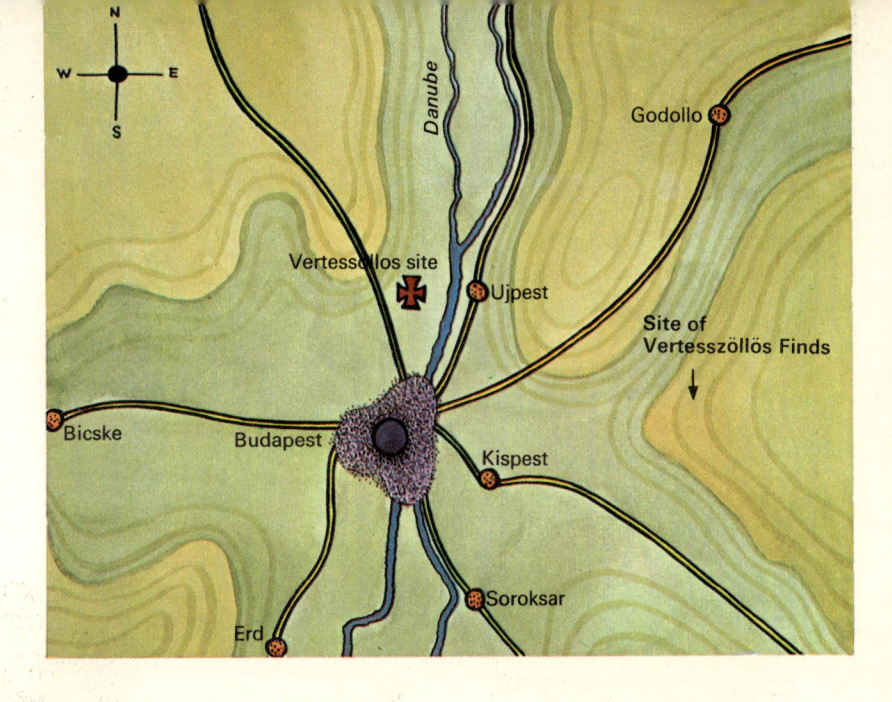

about him, deriving from the massive brow ridges and receding chin.

Somewhat shorter than modern man he was powerfully built. His hands and feet were short. We have direct evidence of the foot size from impressions left in a cave in Italy. All in all, he was not a person with whom to pick a fight.

If he were on the scene today, dressed in modern clothes, he could easily pass unnoticed in a local town. He might earn a few remarks about his rugged looks, but not much more.

His brain size was often larger than that of the average man of today, and he coped well with difficult conditions. As an expert hunter, he killed some of the largest and fiercest animals then living.

Left: The restored skull of a woman found in the Tabūn cave in 1931.

The caves of Mount Carmel – Skūhl and Tabūn – have yielded fossils of two interesting populations. The Tabūn skeleton bears a definite resemblance to Neanderthal, but there are also distinct differences.

The finds in the adjacent cave of Skūhl are considered younger than those of Tabūn – possibly ten thousand years younger. They, too, have some features which could be classed as Neanderthal, though they are more advanced.

These finds support the theory that there were intermediate forms between the classic Neanderthal and modern man.

Above: Neanderthal Man.

The fellow on the left seems to be waving "hello" to those in the foreground, but it may mean instead that he is in mortal danger.

Evidence points to the fact that some Neanderthal hunters took part in cannibalistic feasts at certain times of the year or on special occasions.

Also, a scarcity of food and fierce hunger probably drove the Neanderthal to attack and eat their fellow men.

Their knowledge of fire came in handy at mealtimes whether the main course was man or beast.

His way of life was largely determined by climate, since his span was contemporary with interglacial and glacial periods. In times of extreme cold he lived in caves; at other times he was content to be out in the open. He was able to build himself homes and temporary shelters for hunting.

He hunted most animals. Sometimes he would use snares, sometimes pits, to catch his game. Perhaps he would drive some unfortunate beast over a cliff or make it jump a narrow gorge. In the latter case the weaker animals fell to their death.

Neanderthal man appears to have cut up the animal on the spot and taken the meat back to base camp. The hides were used for clothing – a necessity, especially during the glacial period.

It is in Neanderthal man that we can first detect the beginnings of religion and social feeling.

He buried his dead. The famous find at Le Moustier, France, had a very young man laid carefully on his side, as though asleep. In the grave were a number of flint implements.

Evidence of another burial comes from La Ferrassie in France. Here six people were laid to rest – two adults and four children.

In burying his dead, Neanderthal man was obviously beginning to wonder what death was. Why did people die? What happened to them when they no longer moved about or ate food? Did they cease to exist?

From the positions in which skeletons have been found, it would appear that death was regarded as a form of sleep.

From a cave in Switzerland came the first evidence of a bear cult among at least *some* Neanderthal men. The cave is called Drachenloch (Dragon's Hole). When it was excavated, a bear skull was found arranged with several other bones, all from different cave bears. Also, skulls were found stacked in what is best described as a stone chest. Other such collections have been found in Austria and Germany.

Perhaps they are associated with some form of magic. Here was re-enacted the killing of the cave bear. The bear would have been no easy opponent, standing about one metre above Neanderthal man, on its hind legs. Man certainly needed something to protect him from this beast.

Between 35,000 and 40,000 years ago, these men vanished from the scene, replaced by a more advanced form of man, hardly distinguishable from the men of today. Why they disappeared is not readily understood. Perhaps the newcomer killed the Neanderthalers, or gradually assimilated them by interbreeding. Perhaps modern man stems from Neanderthal.

THE SPREAD OF MODERN MAN

Evidence throughout the Old World of *Homo sapiens sapiens* appears suddenly. Could his origins lie in either Swanscombe or Steinheim ancestors? (Some of these later men existed at the same time as Neanderthal man.)

New stone and bone tools turn up, as if man took a giant leap forward. Various populations seem to be represented.

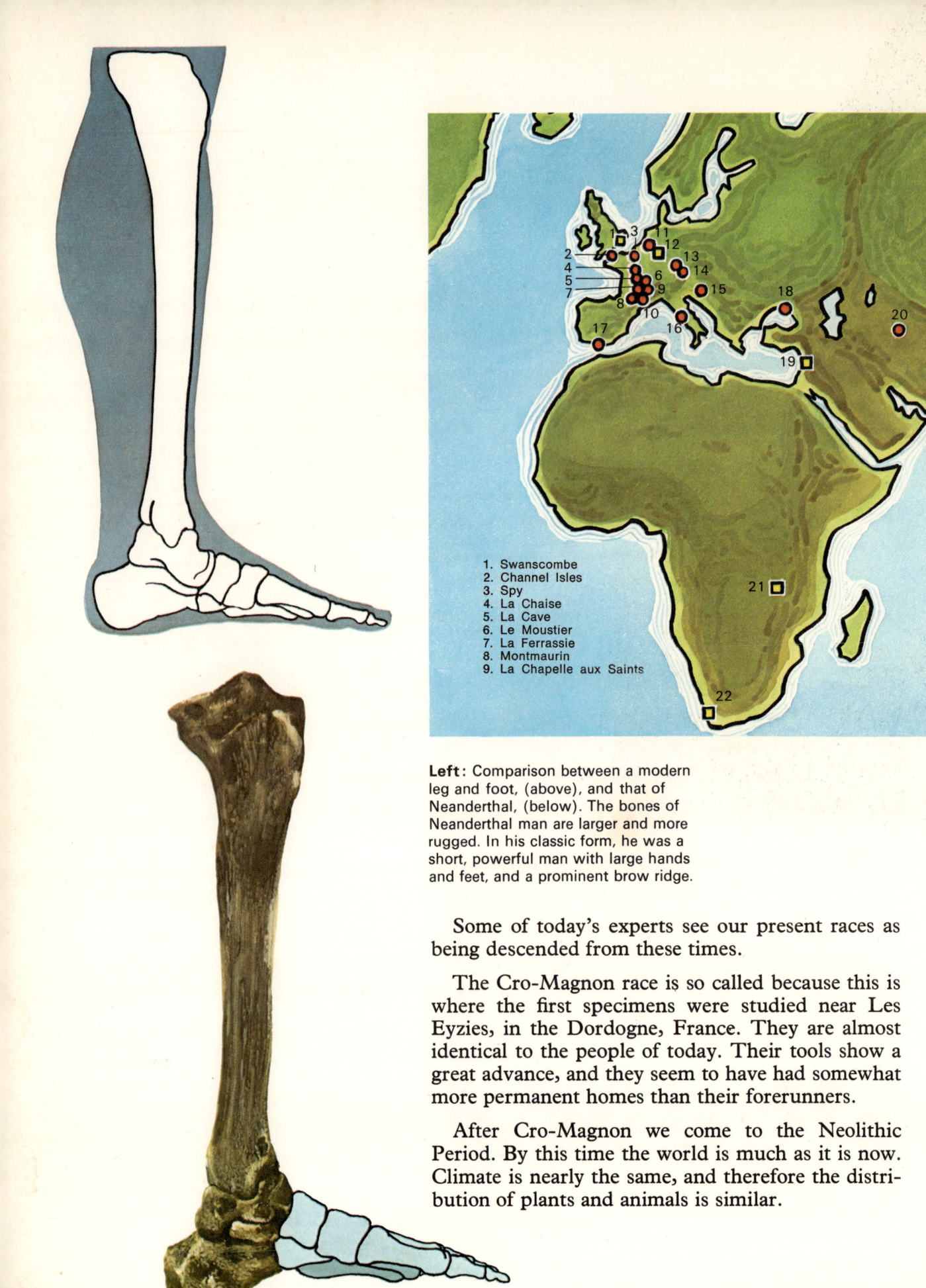

1. Swanscombe
2. Channel Isles
3. Spy
4. La Chaise
5. La Cave
6. Le Moustier
7. La Ferrassie
8. Montmaurin
9. La Chapelle aux Saints

Left: Comparison between a modern leg and foot, (above), and that of Neanderthal, (below). The bones of Neanderthal man are larger and more rugged. In his classic form, he was a short, powerful man with large hands and feet, and a prominent brow ridge.

Some of today's experts see our present races as being descended from these times.

The Cro-Magnon race is so called because this is where the first specimens were studied near Les Eyzies, in the Dordogne, France. They are almost identical to the people of today. Their tools show a great advance, and they seem to have had somewhat more permanent homes than their forerunners.

After Cro-Magnon we come to the Neolithic Period. By this time the world is much as it is now. Climate is nearly the same, and therefore the distribution of plants and animals is similar.

Neanderthal Distribution Map of Neanderthalers and Neanderthaloids

- Neanderthal Sites
- Others

19. Mt. Carmel
20. Teschik-Tasch
21. Broken Hill
22. Saldanha
23. Solo

10. Malarnaud
11. Neanderthal
12. Steinheim
13. Gánovce
14. Sipka
15. Krapina
16. Monte Circeo
17. Gibralter
18. Kiik Koba

Left: Map showing the distribution of classic Neanderthal man, and forms which shared some of the same characteristics, called neanderthaloids. Fossils have been hunted in Europe longer than anywhere else in the world; hence the larger number of finds there. The abundance of Neanderthal finds clouds the true picture of man's evolution. In fact, it is now thought possible that classic Neanderthal man was a dead end in human evolution.

Some of the earlier human skulls tend to be rather long and narrow, while certain skulls of Neolithic age are rounder. The Neolithic skull still tends to be somewhat thicker than that of today.

Until Neolithic times, man was a hunter and a gatherer. He did not have a permanent home. There was no social life, as is the case with, for example, a village existence. Man, of course, was forced to keep on the move to obtain food. As soon as one area became exhausted of suitable game or vegetable food, he moved on to seek new grounds.

In Neolithic times man at last begins to grow food for himself and to tame various animals which will be of use to him.

So begins agriculture. The Middle East would seem to be the home of this vital activity. Here man first grew wheat and barley, and domesticated sheep, goats, and cattle.

This is a most important step in man's evolution. It is from this point that civilization begins.

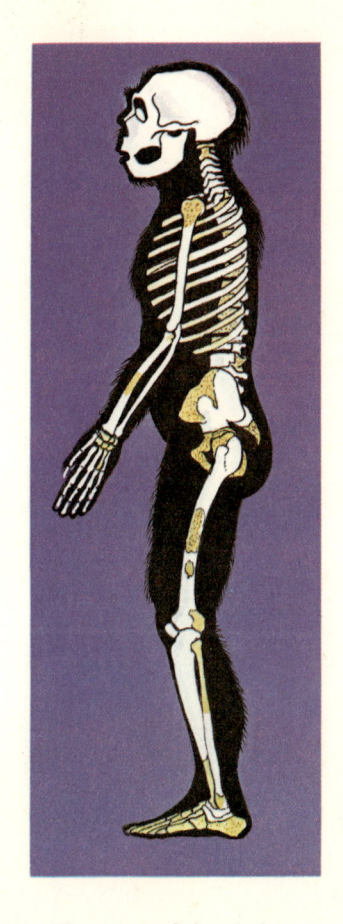

Above: The parts of the skeleton on which was based the original reconstruction of a Neanderthal man came from La Chapelle-aux-Saints.

It has since been proved that the original theory that Neanderthal had a "shuffling walk" is entirely mistaken. Fragments of this original skeleton were later analysed and found to have other characteristics that indicated the man suffered from arthritis. There is no reason to assume that a healthy Neanderthal man could not walk as well as modern man.

Above: Right side view of the skull from Skūhl.

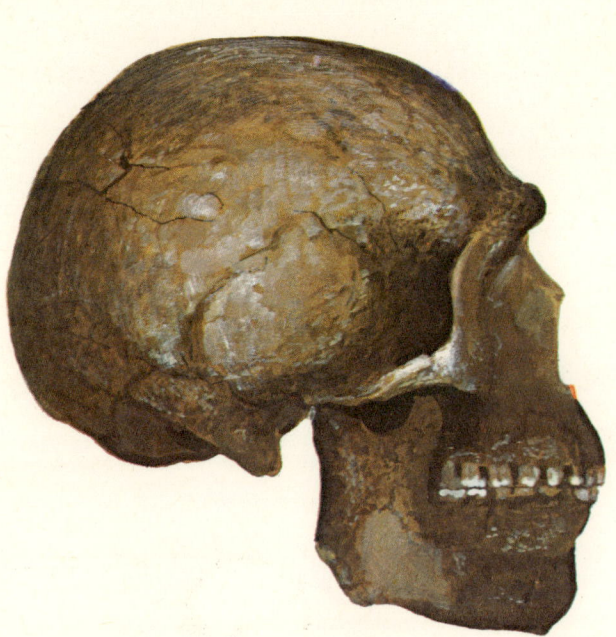

Above right: Left side view of the same skull.
This skull comes from Mugharet es-Skūhl, Mount Carmel, in Israel.
Found with the skull were fossil mammals, including hippopotamus, rhinoceros, hyena, and various forms of deer.
Flint implements have also been found.
The remains from Skūhl show more modern features than those from the neighbouring locality at Tabūn.

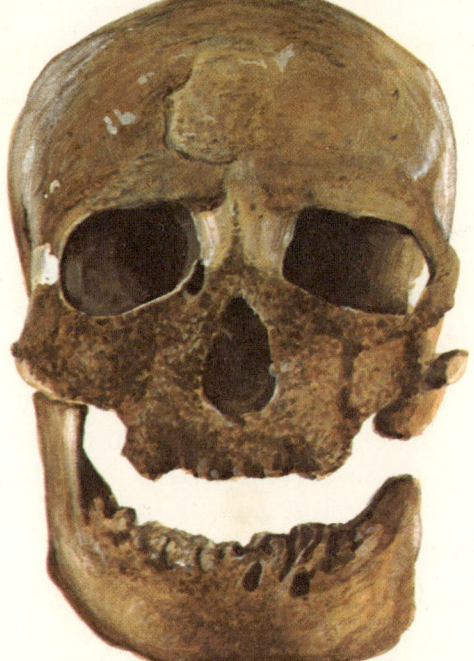

Above: The skull of the "old man" of the Cro-Magnon period.
Found at Cro-Magnon, Les Eyzies, Dordogne, France, in 1868, this is a member of the last "race" of peoples to show any real differences from present day man. One distinctive feature is the long skull.

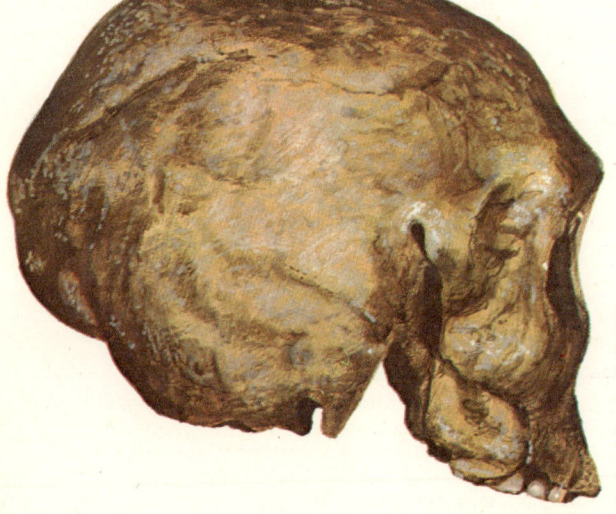

Left: A skull from Wadjak in Java — an example of modern man. It has been suggested that this skull is on an evolutionary line which ends with the Australian Aborigines. A skull from the Niah cave, in Borneo, about forty thousand years old, is considered a forerunner of the Aborigines of Tasmania, who are now extinct.

THE CULTURE OF MAN

The physical evolution of man has been studied in some detail, but it is by research into what he did that we are able to understand how his mind developed.

Items made by man are called artifacts. They may be of bone, horn, antler, wood, or stone.

Man's ability to make tools has always been a central theme in any discussion of his evolution. To be able actually to manufacture implements for a preconceived purpose denotes progress. From the earliest tools examined there is a progression to more complicated forms, and eventually from stone to metal. Development, however, was by no means evenly spaced through time.

Many of man's tools, in fact, are obviously fashioned for a purpose and could never be natural productions. The function of the tool can often be immediately deduced.

Man did not suddenly start to manufacture tools, particularly the fine ones that may be displayed in museums. It was a slow beginning, possibly using natural objects or breaking open a stone to obtain a sharp edge. Thus it is very unlikely that man's earliest attempts at toolmaking will be found.

Man's toolmaking could well have been prompted by a change in his diet. When he started to eat meat, he would need to skin and cut up any animal caught, because man does not have the large canine teeth that so many animals do.

Man also most likely used wood to form many tools, and this material has rotted away by now. Perhaps he used a sharp stone to put a point on a stick. Our ideas on man's first steps into technology are therefore largely surmise.

Toolmaking has set man apart from the other animals. Recent studies on such animals as chimpanzees, however, have revealed their ability to use natural objects as tools. It was man's ability to fashion natural objects into things that could do certain jobs which gave him his lead in the animal kingdom.

Most people think of stone tools as being flint

tools. Obviously, however, flint, which is found in Europe in the chalk, was not available to all prehistoric peoples. If it was obtainable, however, it seems that it was used in preference to anything else. It was obtained in the early days from river banks and cliffs. Other rocks used included obsidian (a glassy volcanic rock), greenstone, quartz, quartzite, and granite.

In Neolithic times flint was mined and traded. It had become a very valuable commodity. Such mines are known to have existed in Belgium, Sweden, France, Portugal and England.

It was long supposed that it took prehistoric man a great deal of time to manufacture his tools. But just think of the many thousands of tools that have been discovered and are now housed in museum collections throughout the world. Imagine, also, how many have not been found.

It is all quite picturesque to imagine prehistoric man sitting outside his cave, flaking away, but in fact, the implements were made quickly. Life was not easy for man then, and there would be little spare time.

The speed with which tools can be made has been demonstrated by various well-known authorities on flint implements.

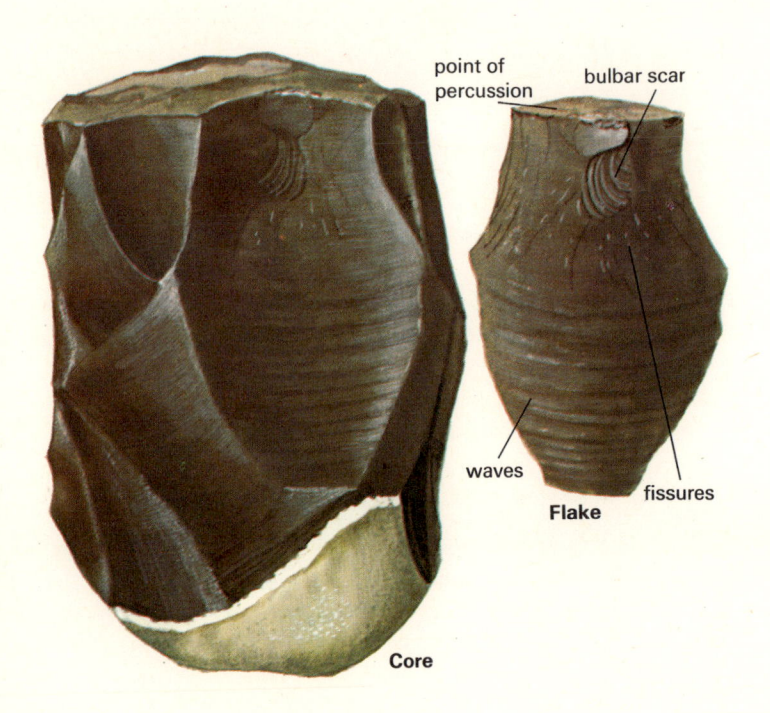

Core

point of percussion
bulbar scar
waves
fissures
Flake

Left: Flint is formed by layer upon layer of a chalky substance being deposited around a hard core. The effect of this "onion-skin" coating is to cause the flint to break into sharp, curved flakes. Often, many small round nodules were bound together to form a large, lumpy flint. When a nodule is broken off, it leaves a smooth round depression with sharp edges.

A flint can be broken like this by a natural rock fall, but we can tell that many flints were broken deliberately into useful shapes. If two rows of adjacent nodules are broken off, they leave a sharp, serrated knife-edge between the two rows of depressions on the remaining mass.

Prehistoric Man became very skilled at breaking flints and shaping them into useful tools. He made "flake tools" from the curved pieces that he chipped off, and "core tools" from the remaining mass.

As time went on his skill became even greater. So we can use some of the tools on a site to estimate its date.

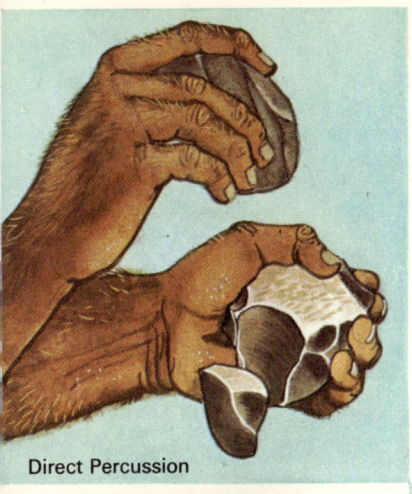

Left: Methods of fashioning implements. In the top line, far left, direct percussion takes place when one stone is used to strike against another. Indirect percussion, shown in the bottom row, far left, leads to a greater degree of precision in flaking. A later development is pressure flaking, and polishing came later still, in the history of man as toolmaker.

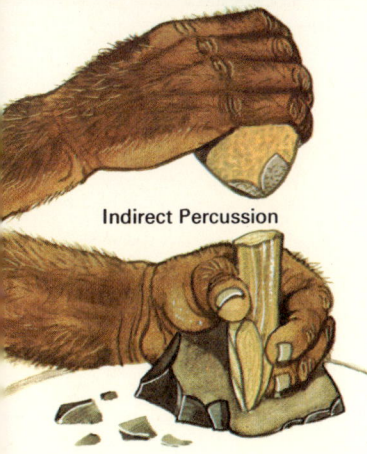

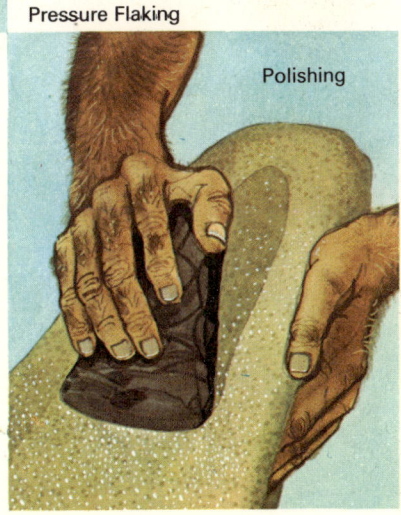

Direct Percussion

Pressure Flaking

Indirect Percussion

Polishing

Right: Some of the earliest tools were flaked in only one or two directions. Many of these shown here have been found in Olduvai Gorge, and the name given to this culture is, appropriately enough, Oldowan.

63

Abbevillian Hand-axe

Acheulean Hand-axes

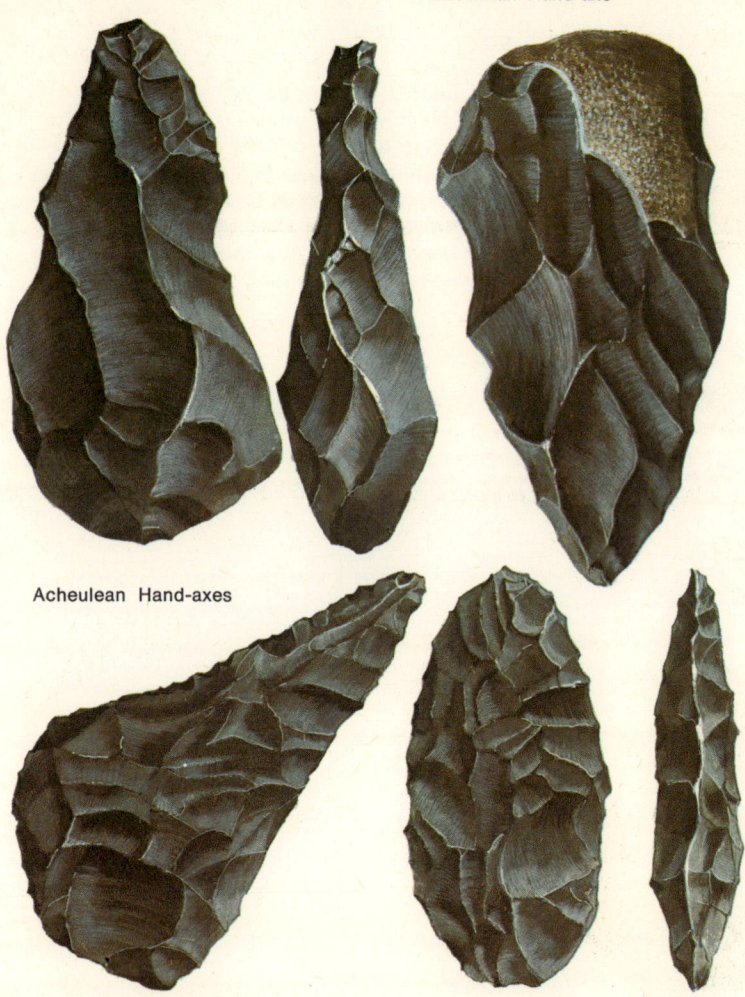

Left: The flaking all around the edge, and the typical pear-shaped result, denote the beginnings of the hand axe culture. It is called Abbevillian.

More refined, with a distinct point and straighter edges, are the hand axes of the more advanced Acheulean stage.

There was a distinct uniformity in prehistoric tools all over the world, even as techniques gradually became more refined, and workmanship improved.

Certain types of tools were common to specific areas, however; for example, the hand axes with an S-shaped border found in France and Britain.

In discussions about the various Stone Age tools, two words are often heard — *industry* and *culture*. The word "culture" in this context refers to all that a particular human society produces. In the case of most prehistoric men, the only remains we have of their culture may be their stone tools. An "industry" refers to the work of a single group within a society.

The various phases of the Stone Age are known as the Palaeolithic, or Old Stone Age (which is further subdivided); the Mesolithic; and the Neolithic, or New Stone Age. It was in Neolithic times that man began to cultivate the land and domesticate animals.

In early Palaeolithic times the tools made were relatively simple, although they are unmistakably tools. Sometimes the workmanship is evident on only one side; other times it is on both. These very old tools have been discovered in Olduvai Gorge, and the culture they form is called the Oldowan culture.

This development was followed by the production of the first crude hand axes of the Abbevillian (from Abbeville, northern France), indicating a spread of tools from Africa into Europe.

With the coming of the ice the Abbevillian culture disappeared and the next stage in the evolution of the hand axe is the Acheulean (from St Acheul, Amiens, France), which had a point and relatively straight

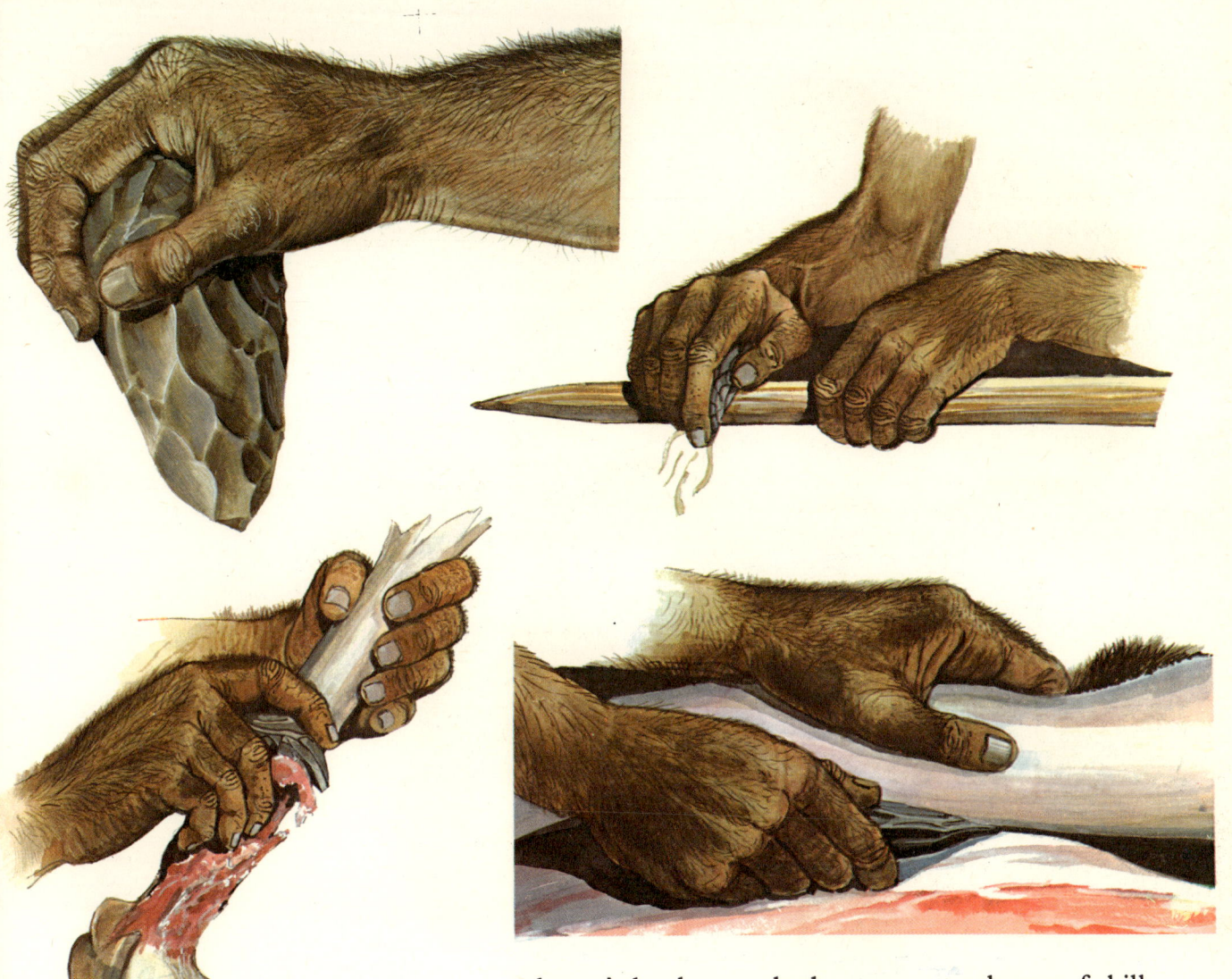

Above: The illustrations show how the hand axe was held and used.

Primitive tools were used to skin animals, to scrape meat from the bones, and to shape wood into other tools. Some of these activities are shown here.

edges. Acheulean tools show a greater degree of skill in manufacture than the earlier tools. An Acheulean hand axe was found near the Swanscombe skull in Kent, England.

Middle Pleistocene men made tools, some of which have been found with *Homo erectus* at Peking. They tend to be rather primitive and could have been the products of either a flake or pebble-tool industry.

Similar industries to this one are also known from India and Java.

Industries which used flake tools are known from Europe. The Clactonian industry is an example. Eastern and central Europe also boast a similar culture called Tayacian (from Tayac, near Les Eyzies, Dordogne, France). This culture is believed by some to have evolved into the Mousterian (after Le Moustier, near Peyzac, Dordogne).

The Mousterian is the culture of Neanderthal man. It has been discovered in Europe, Asia, and

Left: A Mousterian hide scraper. The Mousterian culture is that of the Neanderthal people. They first pegged out the skins and after they were cleaned and dried, used them for clothing during the long periods of cold.

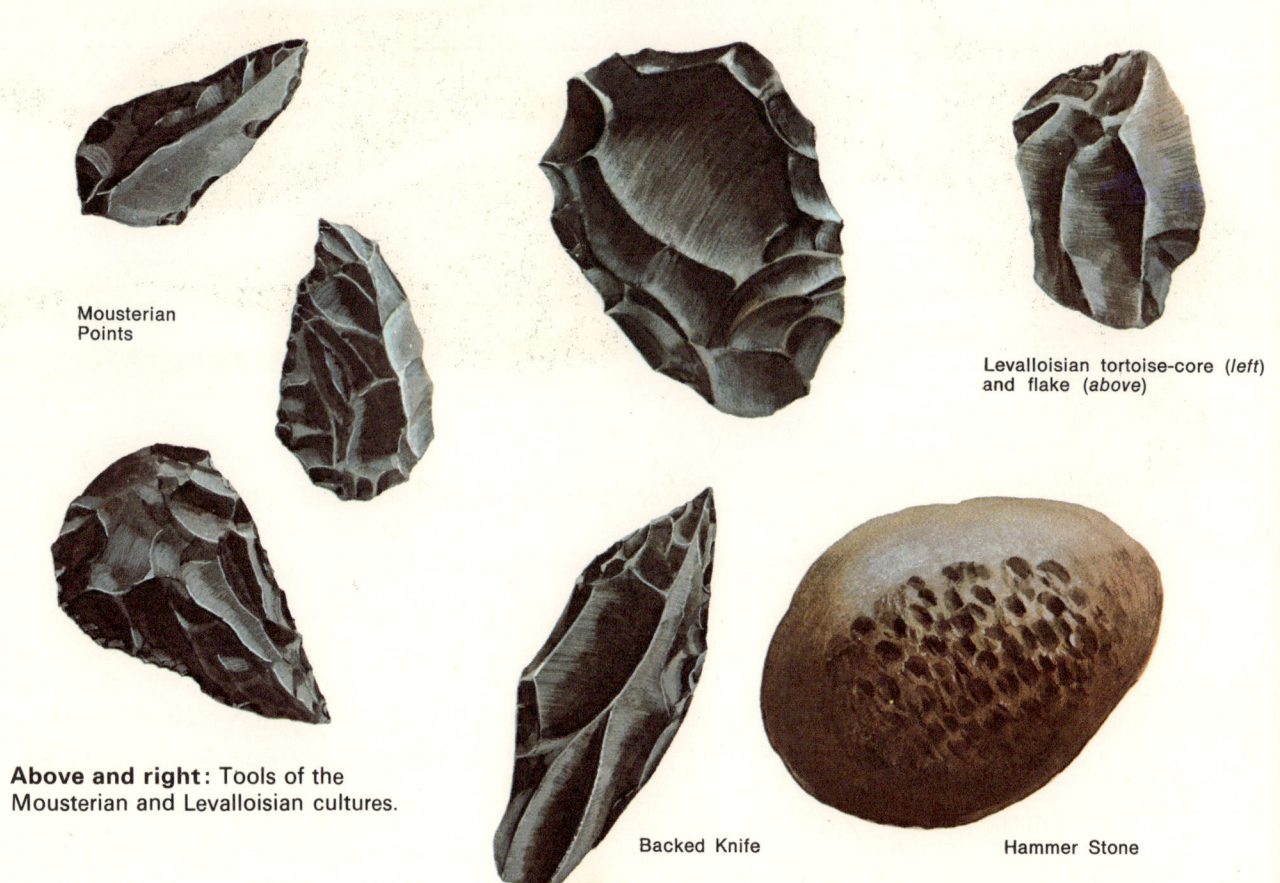

Mousterian Points

Levalloisian tortoise-core (*left*) and flake (*above*)

Above and right: Tools of the Mousterian and Levalloisian cultures.

Backed Knife

Hammer Stone

Africa. The implements may be flakes which have been retouched to make side-scrapers and a triangular point. These tools were most likely used for cutting-up and skinning animals. Some tools would be used in the preparation of the skins. Neanderthal man also had wooden spears.

Late Palaeolithic tools rather abruptly succeed

Left: Cave paintings are among the best-known works of prehistoric man. The earliest ones are thought to originate from the Aurignacian period. During this period, as in the Solutrean and Magdalenian periods, men began to draw, paint, engrave and sculpt, both in bas-relief and in the round. Particularly spectacular examples of cave art are to be found in France and Spain, such as at Altamira and Lascaux.

those of the Mousterian culture in many places. They obviously indicate a new type of man possibly infiltrating from the east. The tools of these new peoples had a wide range, and were capable of working soft stone, wood, or bone. This new culture is characterized by finely-made blades and instruments for engraving, called burins, or gravers. These were used to engrave on bone antler and wood.

The Aurignacian culture (from Aurignac, Toulouse, France) is that of the Cro-Magnon people. The bone industry of these people consists of pins or awls. Points were manufactured for attachment to a shaft, thus forming light spears. The flint industry of this culture includes end-scrapers, trimmed blades and very finely fluted core-like scrapers.

The earliest works of cave art, including some carvings, are attributed to these times.

This culture was followed by the Gravettian (from La Gravette, Couze Valley, south-west France). A narrow, pointed blade, something like a penknife in shape is characteristic. Body painting, too, was practised by this culture, as it most likely was by the Cro-Magnons and the Magdalenians.

The final glaciation came, and with it the Magdalenian culture (from La Madeleine, Tursac, Dordogne, France). The culture has been compared to that of Eskimos.

The flint tools continued to be manufactured, but it was the working of bone, ivory, and antler that set these people apart from the others. Their art is disclosed in the caves of France and Spain, where clay sculptures have also been discovered.

Gravettian Backed Blade

Solutrean Hand Drill

Arrowheads

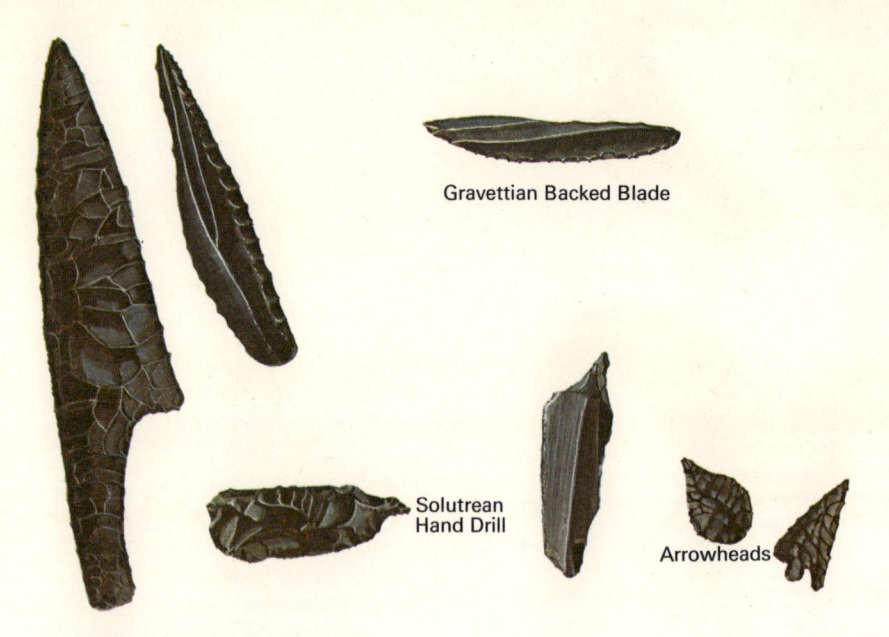

Above: The two large tools are Gravettian points, and to their right is a backed blade of the same culture. Below these are arrowheads and a hand drill, or piercer — representative of the Solutrean culture.

MEN OF THE MIDDLE STONE AGE

As the ice retreated for the last time and the climate became warmer, a new type of culture began to sweep across Europe. These cultures make up the period of time called the Mesolithic.

Tools are still made of stone, but they are characterized by tiny flints called microliths. These were most likely attached to wooden shafts to make effective weapons and hunting tools.

Also belonging to this same period are the kitchen middens, or shell mounds, found in Denmark. Such rubbish heaps reveal, too, much of what Mesolithic men ate. It is obvious from various investigations that they ate a wide variety of foodstuffs, including fish, birds, and mammals.

Right: Tools from the Magdalenian culture. These people, like the Eskimos, made use of bone and antler. They had a great deal in common with the Eskimos, perhaps because they lived in similar surroundings and conditions.

Harpoons and spear points, together with examples of finished sculpture, are shown here.

Above: Solutrean leaf blade. The manufacturers of these fine blades were experts in the field of pressure-flaking, and produced magnificent tools.

Mesolithic men had the ability to manufacture bows and arrows, and to transport themselves along rivers in dug-out canoes. The canoes were made by hollowing out a tree trunk by burning.

MAN BECOMES A FARMER

The Mesolithic Period is followed by the Neolithic stage, or New Stone Age. It had begun in the Middle East some 7,500 years B.C. and it may have had its origins a thousand years earlier.

Gradually the culture was to spread across Europe. Hunting and fishing remained important, during this time. Animals were caught by trap, bow and arrow, and sling. Dogs also helped man, as they had done in the Mesolithic Period.

Fishing was undertaken with hooks and harpoons, both usually made of bone. Nets and traps were used.

The Neolithic Period marks the beginning of agriculture. Wheat and barley were grown. Animals which were domesticated during these times include sheep, goats, cattle, and pigs.

Many new skills had to be learned, such as grinding corn. Baskets were made – and fabrics.

Neolithic men used skin-covered boats, sleds and the earliest known skis.

The wheel seems to have come into use by at least 3000 B.C., again in the Middle East. A wooden cartwheel of about 1900 B.C. has been recovered in the Netherlands.

THE COMING OF METAL

After Neolithic times yet another great change and advance occurred in man's history. Man began to use copper. Thus began the ages of metal. Later man sought out other likely rocks, and by 3000 B.C. bronze was being produced in the Middle East. Tin must have been discovered, since it is tin alloyed with copper which makes bronze.

It should not be imagined that stone tools were immediately replaced by those made of metal. Metal, a scarce commodity, was in great demand for many hundreds of years. Stone tools were thus still manufactured, often in shapes which imitated the much-prized metallic counterparts.

Trade became important. During parts of the

Left: Casting copper.

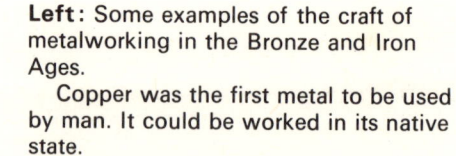

Left: Some examples of the craft of metalworking in the Bronze and Iron Ages.

Copper was the first metal to be used by man. It could be worked in its native state.

At last, man made the great discovery that he could pour molten metal into a prepared mould, thereby casting it into a predetermined shape.

The opportunities seemed unlimited. Soon it was learned that tin and copper could be combined into a much better material for tools and weapons, namely bronze. The name of this new material has been given to a specified span of time in man's development — the Bronze Age.

The new blades, though no sharper than the old flint ones, were less brittle, and more easily sharpened by grinding on a flat stone.

Bronze Age, man in England traded with Ireland, Scandinavia, and the countries to the south.

The soldiers of these times were well-equipped with metal helmets, shields and swords. Women had many forms of jewelry.

Man himself gradually became a specialist. No longer was he an all-purpose beast. Some men specialized in pottery, others tended the forge.

The Bronze Age was followed by the Iron Age. Again the spread was from the east.

It had taken man a long time to learn how to smelt iron ore, but gradually he achieved success and iron tools became a commonplace.

In Britain there are many indications of Iron Age man's occupation. It was brought to a close, however, with the successful Roman invasion; and thus pre-history is turned into history.

Above: More examples of man's prowess in metal working.

Metal came to be used for tools, weapons, and ornaments. Bronze Age axes show a gradual change from simple to more complicated types; there were also daggers, rapiers, hooks, harness pieces, pins and rings. At least one sword has been discovered that is decorated with gold-plated bronze discs.

Swords became longer with the coming of iron, but over the years the blade was gradually shortened.

Other Iron Age artifacts include cauldrons, buckets, helmets, shields, and various pins, including a predecessor of the modern safety pin.

The illustration on the opposite page shows the back of a bronze mirror, dating from Iron Age times.

Above: An Iron Age fort — Maiden Castle, Dorset, England.

The Iron Age people constructed forts on hilltops, and many examples of these still exist. The positions of such forts had obvious military advantages, and the earthworks were most likely surmounted by palisades.

THE RISE OF MAN

We have traced man's history from its beginnings. It is an incomplete story, and many assumptions have had to be made, even to get this far.

Over the years man has come to recognize the true nature of fossils and all that they imply. With the works of Charles Darwin, and many others of the nineteenth century, the foundations for an understanding of man's origins were laid.

In the twentieth century our knowledge has increased by leaps and bounds. Not only have more discoveries been made, but we have learned more of what modern primates are like, and how they live.

By international co-operation and exploration, we shall be able to understand man's evolution fully.

It is appropriate to end by summing-up the findings of an international conference held in 1969 on the origins of *Homo sapiens*, as they affect what has been discussed in the previous pages.

Man in his modern form is now thought to have existed for 60,000 years, instead of the 35,000 to 38,000 years previously estimated.

This would fit in with material from such sites as Swanscombe in Kent and Fontéchevade in France. As well as existing in Europe, such men lived also in Africa and the Middle East.

At this meeting were discussed the various theories on the overall evolution of man. Dr L. S. B. Leakey believes that the genus *Homo* became established in the Lower Pleistocene and that the pithecanthropines and Neanderthal man are but ends in other evolutionary lines.

Others argue that modern man originated in the area of the Middle East and eastern Europe from a form which can best be described as neanderthaloid.

A final group believes that from Middle Pleistocene times onward there was a succession of both neanderthaloid and non-neanderthaloid creatures which evolved to the present day. Not all the branches are represented, now, but some do reach into the present world, represented as the various races of mankind.

Below: A Cro-Magnon group.
In 1886, skeletons of the Late Palaeolithic period were discovered in a cave in Cro-Magnon, hence the name given to the species.
These people were powerful hunters who ate the meat and wore the skins of the animals they killed.

INDEX

Figures in bold type refer to illustrations and captions.

Abbevillian culture, **17**, 64, **64**
Aborigines, **60**
Absolute dating, 17–18
Acheulean culture, **17**, 64–5
Aegyptopithecus, 37
Africa, 9, **35**, **37**, 42–7, **52**, 54, 64, 65, 73
Agriculture, 59, 64, 69
Alaska, 9, 13
Algeria, 51
America (North and South), 6, 7, **8**, **10**, 33, 35
Amphibians, **6**
Apes, 21, 24, 26, 27, 37–8, **42**
Arm, **27**
Artifacts, 61–71
Asia, 7, 9, **37**, 54, 65
Aurignacian culture, **17**, 67, **67**
Australia, 6
Australopithecines, 25, **31**, 34, 38, **42**, **44**, 46, 47, 49, **50**, 51
  gracile, 38, **39**, **40**, **41**, **42**, 43, 44, 45, 47
  robust, **41**, 43, 44
Australopithecus, 42
Australopithecus africanus, 43
Austria, 57

Baboons, 34, **34**
Baccinello Mine (Italy), **37**
Belgium, 62
Bipedalism, 26, 27
Birds, **6**
Bison, **8**
Black's Tooth, **46**, **47**, **48**
Bones, 49
  composition, 22–3
  fossils *see* Fossil bones
  structure, 23, **23**
  see also under specific names
Borneo, **60**
Botanical analysis, 16–17
Brain, 24, **24**, 30–1, **31**, 49
Britain, **64**, 71
  Roman invasion, 71
Bronze, 69
Bronze Age, **70**, 71, **71**
Burins, 67
Bush babies, 34

Caeonozoic Era, **6**, 27
Cambrian Period, **6**, 9
Canaliculi, 23
Carbon-14 dating, 18, **19**
Carboniferous Period, **6**
Carnivores, **32**
Carpals, **27**
Cave
  paintings, 67, **67**
  sites, **13**, 15, **42**
Cerebrum, **31**
Cerebral hemispheres, **31**
Chellean culture, **17**
Chimpanzee, **31**, 34, **35**, 38, 41, 61
China, 38

Choukoutien, **46**, **47**
Clactonian culture, 65
Classification of man, 32–5
Clavicle (collar bone), **27**
Clay sculpture, 67
Continental drift, 7
Copper, 69, **70**
Cores, **21**, **62**
Cranium, **24**
Cretaceous Period, **6**, **32**, **33**, 35
Cro-Magnon man, 58, **60**, 67, **72**
Culture 61–71
  see also under names

Dart, Prof. R., **38**
Darwin, Charles, 72
Dating finds, 15, 16–21, 41
Deer, 9, **47**, **60**
Deinotherium, **10**
Dendrochronology, 18, **19**
Denmark, **12**
Dentition
  see Teeth
Devonian Period, **6**
Dinosaurs, 35
Drachenloch (Switzerland), 57
Dryopithecines, 38
Dryopithecus, 37
Dubois, Eugene, 47, 51

Early Palaeolithic Period, **17**, 64
Egypt, 37
Elephants, **9**, 31
England, 62, 71
Eocene Period, **6**, **32**, **33**, 35, 36
Eskimos, 67, **68**
Europe, 7, 9, **37**, 38, 41, 53, **58**, 64, 65, 73
Excavation, 15

Far East, **35**, 47, 52
Faroes, 6
Fayum (Egypt), 37
Femur, **26**
Fibula, **26**
Fire, 49, **50**
Fishes, **6**
Fishing, 69
Fission tracks, **21**
Flake tools, **62**, **63**, **64**, 65
Flint tools, 57, 61–2, **62**
Fluorine dating, 16, 17
Foot, **26**, **29**, **58**
Foramen magnum, **24**, 27
Forest, **36**
Fossil bones, 15–16, **15**, **58**, **72**
  Preservation, 15–16, 45, **45**
Fossilization, 11–15, **11**, **12**, **13**
France, 57, 58, 62, 67, 73

Geochronology, 16
Geological time scale, **6**
Germany, 57
Gibbon, **31**, 34, **35**, 38
Gigantopithecus, 38
Glacial and interglacial periods, 7, 8–10, **8**, **9**
Glaciers, 7, 8
Gorilla, 24, 28, **34**, **35**, 38, 41
Gravettian culture, 67, **68**

Great Britain, 9
Great Ice Age, 7
Great Rift Valley
  see Olduvai Gorge
Greenland, 6
Grip, **28**
Günz glaciation, **7**, 20
Günz-Mindel interglacial, **7**, 20

Hand axes, 64, **64**, 65, **65**
Hand bones, **27**, 30
Haversian canals, 23
Hedgehog, 36
Heidelberg remains, 51, **51**
Hill forts, 71
Hip bone, **41**
Hippopotamus, 9, 60
Holocene (Recent) Period, 20
Hominids, **6**, 34, 38, 39, 42–4
Homo, 34, 49, 73
Homo erectus, **31**, 47, **47**, **50**, 51, 52, **53**, 65
Homo habilis, **46**, **47**
Homo pekinensis, **46**, 47, **47**, **48**, **50**, 51, 65
Homo sapiens, 34, 52, 72
Homo sapiens neanderthalensis, 34, 52–7, **56**, **58**, 65, 66, **66**, 73
Homo sapiens sapiens, 34, 57–9
Horses, **8**
Humerus, **27**
Hyena, **60**

Ice sheets, **6**
India, **35**, 38, 65
Insectivores, **32**, **33**, 36
Interglacial periods, *see* Glacial and interglacial periods
Interpluvials, 9
Intrusive burial, **18**
Invertebrates, **6**, 32
Iraq, 54
Ireland, 71
Iron Age, **70**, 71, **71**
Isotopic dating, 18, **18**, 20
Israel, 54
Italy, 37, 55

Java remains, 47, **48**, 51, **60**, 65
Jaws, **25**, **43**, **50**, **51**
  see Mandible *and* Maxillae
Jewelry, 71
Jurassic, **6**

Kanapoi (Kenya), 45
Kenya, 38
Koenigswald, Prof. von, **50**, 51
Kromdraai remains, **38**, 44

Laboratory work, **14**, **16**
La Chapelle aux Saints, **57**
Lacunae, 23
La Ferrassie, 57
Lamellae, 23
Land plants, **6**
Late Carboniferous, 9
Late Palaeolithic Age, **17**, 66–7
Leakey, Dr. L. S. B., 45–6, 73

Leakey, Dr. Mary, **44**, 45–6
Leakey, Richard, 47
Leg bones, **26**, **49**, **58**
Lemurs, **33**, **34**, **35**
Les Eyzies (France), 58, **60**
Levalloisian culture, **17**, **66**
Limestone, 13
Lion, **9**
Lorises, **34**
Lothagam Hill (Sudan) remains, 45

Magdalenian culture **17**, 67, **68**
Maiden castle, England, **71**
Makapansgat remains, **38**, 44
Mammals, **6**, 32–4, **32**, 35, **55**, **60**
Mammoth, **8**, 13
Mandible, **24**, **63**
Maxillae, 24
Mesolithic Period, **17**, 64, 68–9
Mesozoic Era, **6**, 35
Metacarpals, **27**
Metal, 69–71
Metatarsals, **26**
Microliths, 68
Middle East, 54, 59, 69, 73
Middle Palaeolithic Age **17**
Middle Stone Age, *see* Mesolithic Period
Mindel glaciation, **7**, 20
Mindel-Riss interglacial, **7**, 20, **54**
Miocene Period, **6**, **32**, **36**, 37
Modern man, 34, 40, 47, 52–61, **53**, **60**, 72–3
 structure of, 22–31
Modjokerto remains, **48**, **50**
Monkeys, 34, **34**, **35**
Morocco remains, 51, 52
Mount Carmel remains, 54
Mousterian culture, **17**, 57, 65–7, **66**

Natron remains, **44**
Neanderthal man, *see Homo sapiens neanderthalensis*
Neanderthal remains, 52–7
Neolithic culture, **17**, 62
Neolithic Period, **17**, 58–9, 64, 69
New Stone Age *see* Neolithic Period
New World monkeys, 36
New Zealand, 7
Ngandong remains, **48**
Notharctus, **35**

Occipital, **24**
Oldowan culture, **17**, **63**, 64
Old Stone Age *see* Palaeolithic Age
Olduvai Gorge (Tanzania), 20, 29, **44**, 45–7, **45**, 51, **53**, **63**, 64
Old World monkeys, 36–7
Oligocene Period, **6**, **32**, 36, 37
Omo remains (Ethiopia), 45
Orang-utan, 34, **35**
Ordovician Period, **6**
Oreopithecus, 37, **37**

Palaeolithic Age, **17**, 64, 72
Palaeolithic Age tools, 64–7
Palaeontologists, 15

Palaeozoic Era, **6**
Palaeocene Period, **6**, **32**, 36
Pangea, 7
Paranthropus, 43
Pebble tools, 65
Peking remains, **46**, 47, **47**, **48**, **50**, 51, 65
Pelvis, 28–9, **30**, **40**, **41**
Peninj (Tanzania), **44**, 47
Perigordian culture, **17**
Permian, **6**
Phalanges, **26**, **27**
Piltdown man, 39–40
Pithecanthropines, 47–51, **48**, **52**, **53**, 73
Pleistocene Period, **6**, 7–10, **7**, **10**, 16, 20, **32**, 38
 Lower, 7, 20, 73
 Middle, 7, 20, 47, 65, 73
 Upper, 7, 20, 47–51
Pliocene Period, **6**, 20, **32**, **37**, 38, **54**
Pluvial and interpluvial periods, 9
Pollen dating, 16
Portugal, 62
Potassium-argon dating, 20
Pottery, 71
Pre-Cambrian Period, **6**, 9
Primates, **6**, 22, 24, 26, 27, **32**, 34–7, 41
 distribution, **33**, **35**
 evolution, 33, 36
 migration, **33**
Proconsul africanus, **36**, **37**
Propliopithecus, 37

Radioactive dating, 18–20
Radius, **27**
Ramapithecus, 37, 38, 39
Rancho La Brea, **10**, 13
Reindeer, **8**
Relative dating, 13–14, 16–17, **47**
Religion, 56–7
Reptiles, **6**, 35
Rhinoceros, **8**, **9**, 60
Riss glaciation, **7**, 20
Riss-Würm interglacial, **7**, 20
River terrace, **8**
Rodents, **32**, 36
Rudolf, Lake, remains, 47
Rusinga Island (Kenya), **37**

Sabre-toothed tiger, **10**
Sangiran remains, **48**, **50**
Scandinavia, **8**, 71
Scapulae, **27**
Sea weeds, **6**
Shell mounds, 68
Siberia, 13
Silurian Period, **6**, 47
Sinanthropus pekinensis, 47
Skeleton, 22–30, **22**, **59**
Skūhl remains, 54, **55**, **60**
Skull, 24, **24**, **40**, **41**, **43**, 46, **48**, **49**, **50**, **53**, **54**, **55**, **56**, 57, 59, **60**
Soldiers, 71
Solutrean culture, **17**, **68**
South Africa, Rep. of, **38**, **39**, 40, **40**, **41**, **42**, 44
Spain, 67
Steinheim remains, 52, **53**, 57
Sterkfontein remains, **38**, **41**, 44
Stone Age, 64–9
Stratigraphy, 16
Swanscombe remains, 52, **53**, **54**, 57, 65, 73

Swartkrans remains, **38**, **41**, 44, 47, 51, **53**
Sweden, **17**, 62
Switzerland, 57

Tabūn remains, 54, **55**, **60**
Tarsals, **26**
Tarsiers, 34, **34**
Taung remains (South Africa), **38**, **39**, 44
Tayacian culture, 65
Teeth, 23, 24–5, **25**, **47**, 51, **56**
Ternifine remains, **52**
Tibia, **26**
Tiger, Sabre-toothed, **10**
Tin, 69, **70**
Tools, 44, **47**, 49, 57, 58, 61–71
 Abbevillian, **17**, **64**, 64
 Acheulian, **17**, **45**, 64
 Aurignacian, **17**, 67, **67**
 Bone tools, 57, 67, **68**
 Bronze, 69, **70**, **71**
 Chellean, **17**, **45**
 Clactonian, 65
 Copper, 69, **70**
 Gravettian, 67, **68**
 Iron, **70**, 71
 Levalloisian, **17**, **66**
 Magdalenian, **17**, 67, **68**
 Metal tools, 69, 71
 Mousterian, **17**, 65–7, **66**
 Neolithic, **17**
 Oldowan, 17, 45, 63, **63**
 Perigordian, **17**
 Solutrean, **17**, **68**
 Stone tools, 57, 61–9
 Tayacian, 65
Trade, 71
Tree ring counting, **19**
Tree shrew, **33**, **34**, **35**
Triassic Period, **6**, **32**
Trinil remains, **48**, **49**

Ukraine, 13–14
Ulna, **27**
Uranium dating, 20

Varves, **17**
Vertebrae, **23**, **28**
Vertebral column (spine), **23**
Vertebrates, **6**, 22, 32
Vertesszöllös remains, 52, **54**, **55**
Vikings, 6
Villafranchian Period, **20**

Walking, 29, **30**
Weapons, **70**, 71, **71**
Whales, 31
Wolf, **8**
Würm glaciation, **7**, 20
Würm interglacial, **7**

Zinjanthropus, **44**, **46**